"Nancy Monelli is a gifted writer whose insightful prose and heartfelt stories awaken us to the need for deeper truth and greater humility. This book shines a light on what truly matters and what endures. With clarity and grace, Nancy illuminates Scripture in a way that nourishes, comforts, and heals. Her words are food for the soul—and when paired with your action, they will fill you with truth, hope, and joy, even in a troubled and suffering world."

—CAMILLE MCGEE, Wise Elder

"We owe Nancy Monelli a debt of gratitude for offering up a rich gift. Drawing upon the deep well of Scripture, personal experience, stories, and wisdom from the communion of saints, Nancy provides an in-depth exploration of the venerable prayer of St. Francis. She does this not through analysis or explanation but by helping the reader to pray the prayer! My advice? Take it slowly. Treat it as a retreat. Commit to a chapter a day or one a week, either alone or with others. *Lord, Make Us Instruments of Your Peace* is a valuable tool for forming faith."

—BRYON HANSEN, Pastor, First Lutheran Church of West Seattle

"This book is such a gift when you feel overwhelmed, with too many things competing for your time, energy, attention. Here is a prayer discipline that is beautiful in its brevity and simplicity. It gently guides us to explore, one line at a time, the profound and transformative wisdom of this beloved traditional prayer. This lovely book invites us to take back a moment to listen to our true calling as Christians."
—JOHANNA EBY, Neurodiversity Support Specialist and Care Advocate

"This book guides readers through a thoughtful exploration of the Prayer attributed to St. Francis as a way to deepen our spiritual lives. The author includes self-examination, Scripture readings, prayer, and imagination to help uncover our relationship to each pair of concepts—hatred-love, injury-pardon, etc. The pacing of the book allows for reflection and contemplation, encouraging readers to follow Jesus' teachings actively. It is a treasure of inspiration and compassion."
—GINGER HARSTAD GLAWE, Clinical Psychologist

*Lord, Make Us Instruments
of Your Peace*

Lord, Make Us Instruments of Your Peace

An Experience with Prayer in Action and Action in Prayer

NANCY MONELLI

WIPF & STOCK · Eugene, Oregon

LORD, MAKE US INSTRUMENTS OF YOUR PEACE
An Experience with Prayer in Action and Action in Prayer

Copyright © 2025 Nancy Monelli. All rights reserved. Except for brief quotations in critical publications or reviews, no part of this book may be reproduced in any manner without prior written permission from the publisher. Write: Permissions, Wipf and Stock Publishers, 199 W. 8th Ave., Suite 3, Eugene, OR 97401.

Wipf & Stock
An Imprint of Wipf and Stock Publishers
199 W. 8th Ave., Suite 3
Eugene, OR 97401

www.wipfandstock.com

PAPERBACK ISBN: 979-8-3852-6162-8
HARDCOVER ISBN: 979-8-3852-6163-5
EBOOK ISBN: 979-8-3852-6164-2

11/05/25

Scripture quotations are from the New Revised Standard Version Bible, copyright © 1989 National Council of the Churches of Christ in the United States of America. Used by permission. All rights reserved worldwide.

To the glory of God and in thanksgiving for the support and encouragement of Roy Mock, Jessie Williams, Camille McGee, and Pastor Bryon Hansen

Contents

The Prayer Attributed to St. Francis | ix

A Quick Caveat | xi

Introduction: Lord, Make Us Instruments of Your Peace | xiii

1. Where There Is Hatred, Let Us Sow Love | 1
2. Where There Is Injury, Pardon | 10
3. Where There Is Discord, Union | 23
4. Where There Is Doubt, Faith | 31
5. Where There Is Despair, Hope | 40
6. Where There Is Darkness, Light | 47
7. Where There Is Sadness, Joy | 53
8. Grant That We May Not So Much Seek to Be Consoled as to Console; to Be Understood as to Understand; to Be Loved as to Love | 61
9. For It Is in Giving That We Receive; It Is in Pardoning That We Are Pardoned; and It Is in Dying That We Are Born to Eternal Life | 68
10. Amen: Some Closing Thoughts | 74

Bibliography | 83

The Prayer Attributed to St. Francis

TRADITIONAL VERSION

Lord, make me an instrument of Your peace;
Where there is hatred, let me sow love;
Where there is injury, pardon;
Where there is doubt, faith;
Where there is despair, hope;
Where there is darkness, light;
And where there is sadness, joy.

O Divine Master,
Grant that I may not so much seek
To be consoled as to console;
To be understood, as to understand;
To be loved, as to love;
For it is in giving that we receive,
It is in pardoning that we are pardoned,
And it is in dying that we are born to Eternal Life.
Amen.[1]

---

1. Nerburn, *Make Me an Instrument*, ix.

THE PRAYER ATTRIBUTED TO ST. FRANCIS

BOOK OF COMMON PRAYER VERSION

Lord, make us instruments of your peace.
Where there is hatred, let us sow love;
where there is injury, pardon;
where there is discord, union;
where there is doubt, faith;
where there is despair, hope;
where there is darkness, light;
where there is sadness, joy.

Grant that we may not so much seek to
be consoled as to console;
to be understood as to understand;
to be loved as to love.
For it is in giving that we receive;
it is in pardoning that we are pardoned;
and it is in dying that we are born to eternal life. *Amen.*[2]

---

2. *Book of Common Prayer*, 822.

A Quick Caveat

This prayer, long attributed to St. Francis of Assisi (1181–1226), cannot be found in any of the beloved saint's writings. In fact, it can only be traced as far back as 1912. At that time, it appeared in French in *La Clochette*, a small spiritual publication of the Parisian Catholic organization La Ligue de la Sainte-Messe. It was originally titled "A Beautiful Prayer to Say During the Mass" and was not attributed to any author. This, however, was just the beginning of the prayer's long journey to becoming the much-loved prayer attributed to St. Francis. In 1915 this French prayer was sent to Pope Benedict XV and a year later it appeared, translated into Italian, in the Vatican's daily newspaper. A few years after that, a Franciscan priest published the French version on the back of a prayer card that bore the image of St. Francis. Now it carried the title "Prayer for Peace" but was still not attributed to St. Francis. The first time his name was attached to the prayer was in 1927 when it was circulated by the French Protestant group known as the Knights of the Prince of Peace. The first known English translation was also attributed to St. Francis and appeared in the book *Living Courageously*, published in 1937 by Kirby Page. From the time of World War II forward, the prayer was widely circulated and always credited to St. Francis. In the United States, the prayer became known primarily through the books of Cardinal Francis Joseph Spellman, who was the archbishop of New York from 1939 until 1967.[1]

---

1. Christianity.com Editorial Staff, "What Is the Prayer."

A QUICK CAVEAT

Neither the Franciscan order nor scholars attribute this prayer to St. Francis. The Franciscans note that, among other things, the use of the first-person singular pronouns ("I," "me") is self-oriented and not typical of the saint's other writings.[2] That being said, most of the theology of this prayer, especially when prayed with the words "us" and "we" replacing "I" and "me," seems in keeping with Francis's rule of life. This was a man, after all, who referred to all creatures as his brothers and sisters and lived a life of self-imposed poverty so that he could be free to serve Jesus by sharing the gospel and caring for others unfettered by the trappings of personal possessions. For the purposes of this publication, therefore, the prayer will be referred to as "the Prayer Attributed to St. Francis," or simply "the Prayer of St. Francis."

2. Renoux, "Origin."

Introduction

Lord, Make Us Instruments of Your Peace

The purpose of this book is to help you use the Prayer of St. Francis to explore—in an active, lived-out way—what it means to follow Jesus both as an individual and as a member of the body of Christ.

Each time we pray the Lord's Prayer, we ask for God's kingdom to "come on earth as it is in heaven" (Matt 6:9–13). We pray these words, I believe, not just in hope of God's future action on our behalf, but also as a reminder that God has already given us the gifts we need to live as if this time has already come. These gifts include the universal gifts of salvation and a renewed relationship with God through the mediation of Jesus and the power of the Holy Spirit as well as the unique gifts of the Holy Spirit given to each individual.

When we use these gifts and live as God's people in the ways of God's kingdom, we also share glimpses of what life in God's eternal kingdom will look like when it is fully accomplished. And we do this not just with and for our fellow believers but for everyone else as well. By looking to the life of Jesus and his teachings, as well as the lives lived by members of the church throughout history, we can begin to see and live into a life in God's kingdom right here and right now. When we actively pray the Prayer Attributed to St. Francis, open to its instruction, we can open ourselves to the guidance of the Holy Spirit as we seek to live kingdom lives.

INTRODUCTION

For the purposes of this experience, I have chosen to use the version of this prayer that is found in the Book of Common Prayer. It is a prayer for the entire community rather than just an individual. While the prayer as an individual plea is important, and one I feel led to use often in my own devotions, this communal version reminds us of our interconnectedness and our need to pray for and with each other as we seek to inhabit God's kingdom here on earth as it is in heaven. Please note the grammatical difference between the two prayers as well: in the version for individuals, the first phrase ends with a semicolon ("Lord, make me an instrument of Your peace;"), making *peace* the first in a list of desired behaviors. In the communal version, this same phrase ends with a period. It is the first complete thought of the prayer. This small but important distinction implies that all the lines following the first sentence are the actions needed to fulfill it. This expression of the prayer seems to say that if we want to be *instruments of God's peace*, to live as residents of God's kingdom, we can only do so by offering love, pardon, unity, light, hope, and joy where there is hatred, discord, doubt, despair, darkness, and sadness. And we can only live this way through the gift of God's grace.

Thus the prayer begins: "Lord, make us instruments of Your peace." It is to this peace that we are called. This is the peace of shalom. The Holy Scriptures use the word *shalom* to mean more than just the absence of conflict, although it does mean that as well. Shalom, however, is also used to mean "well-being, wholeness, the perfection of God's creation, and abundance."[1] As the prayer continues, it details the essence of what it means to be an instrument of such peace. It expresses the deep desire to be an active participant in God's kingdom of shalom by sowing the seeds of love, pardon, faith, hope, light, and joy in one's own life and to do so by living in a self-sacrificing way that offers consolation, understanding, love, and generosity to others.

This prayer asks God to grant us the ability to live in the kingdom of God through God's mercy and grace. According to missiologist and author Al Tizon, the church moves toward this

---

1. Harper, *Very Good Gospel*, 12.

INTRODUCTION

kind of kingdom living when, as individuals and a body, they are intentionally committed to becoming a "Christ-centered, Spirit-empowered community, wherein they embody righteousness, compassion, love, justice, and peace—shalom—as a model for the whole world."[2]

This book and the activities it encourages is designed for those who would like to pray this prayer with the expectation that the Holy Spirit will empower them to live it out in their own lives and the lives of their faith communities.

Each chapter will lead you through a contemplative and biblically based interaction with the prayer, followed by suggestions for actions you can take to help you live out what you have learned. I encourage you to reach out to others to help you on this journey. This may be as simple as asking for prayers or talking with others about what you are learning and experiencing. I also encourage you to invite others to join you in some of the suggested activities. This may seem difficult at first, but by including others on your journey with this prayer, you will discover a deeper connection to your community of faith and increased abilities to live and serve in God's kingdom of shalom.

This book is not intended to be a "quick read," nor is it a scholarly examination of the theology of St. Francis or the actual author of this prayer. This book is intended to help you live more fully as a follower of Jesus in the specific context of your life and the life of your community of faith. It will not give you answers but it will inspire you to ask important questions and take risks as you seek to answer them.

I pray that this entire process will lead you into a deeper understanding of just what God's kingdom, the kingdom of shalom, can look like as sparks of its light appear in the world in ways both big and small. Please use this book as the Spirit and your schedule allow. Take as much or as little time as you need to read each chapter and experience the activities. There is no expiration date on our spiritual journeys and there is no need to rush through this leg of it either.

2. Tizon, *Whole and Reconciled*, 116.

INTRODUCTION

My hope is that each time you pick up this book, you will do so prayerfully and with a sense of curiosity and humility. I pray that this entire process will lead you into a deeper understanding of just what God's kingdom can look like as it appears in the world, in ways both big and small.

It is important to remember, as we read, pray, and actively engage with the petitions of this prayer, that we are not asking to become saviors. Jesus is the only savior we (or the rest of the world) need. The prayer does not ask God to make us into superheroes who solve all the problems of the world. Rather, this prayer and this book are about helping us to step boldly into kingdom living in small ways. Will our lives change and will we grow because of the prayers we pray and the work we do? I sincerely hope so. But in the prayer, we petition God to help us sow rather than reap in the hope and confidence that God will bring growth to what we have planted. "Sowing does not imply that something is fully grown, only that the seeds of possibility have been planted."[3] We ask only to sow and then pray that God will use what we have planted. Perhaps then we can one day look back on our lives and reflect on who we've become and what we have done in much the same way that Paul did when he wrote: "I planted, Apollos watered, but God gave the growth" (1 Cor 3:6).

> *May the creative power of the Father, the redeeming love of the Son, and the empowerment of the Holy Spirit guide you on this journey into the kingdom of shalom today and forevermore. Amen.*

---

3. Nerburn, *Make Me an Instrument*, 32.

1

Where There Is Hatred, Let Us Sow Love

Let no man pull you so low as to hate him.
—Martin Luther King Jr.

Hate, it has caused a lot of problems in this world, but has not solved one yet.
—Maya Angelou

FOUNDATION

Let us begin our journey with a brief exploration of what we mean when we use the word *love*.

In English love can mean a variety of things, depending upon the context in which it is used. It can describe a sentiment that implies a fondness for another or it can be employed as a way of explaining how much we enjoy the experience of a specific activity or sensation such as the taste of a particular food while we eat. Love can imply anything from a physical attraction toward a specific person to a universal acceptance of all people.

In Hebrew, the word אַהֲבָה (in its various forms) conveys a variety of meanings, similarly to the way the word "love" does in English. But in Greek, the language the New Testament was originally written in, there are different words for each kind of love that is being described. There is a word for self-love, a word for love in friendship, and a word for passionate love, to list a few. The New Testament uses the Greek word *agapē* to describe the kind of self-giving love that comes from God. Agape is also used to describe the kind of love that we, as followers of Jesus, are called to share. This kind of love requires action rather than mere feeling; it is a love that is not dependent upon how lovable (or not) the recipient of this love is. Therefore, agape tells us much more about the one offering love than the one who receives it. When God offers us this love, we receive the joy of seeing the very essence of God and how God acts. As the Scriptures remind us, time and again, God's love for us has never been something we have earned or deserved. "God proves his love [agape] for us in that while we still were sinners Christ died for us" (Rom 5:8). The love God shares with us, therefore, is an aspect of God's very nature. And we are called by Jesus to become people of love, people who love in the way God loves.

> This is my commandment, that you love [agape] one another as I have loved you. (John 15:12)

In order to sow love, we must become people who love, regardless of the nature or behavior of those we are called to love.

> You have heard that it was said, "You shall love your neighbor and hate your enemy." But I say to you, love your enemies and pray for those who persecute you, so that you may be children of your Father in heaven; for he makes his sun rise on the evil and on the good, and sends rain on the righteous and on the unrighteous. (Matt 5:43–46)

Our plea to sow love where there is hate must first become a prayer. We should ask God to transform us into loving people regardless of how others treat us or those we love. We must pray for the grace to love as God loves: personally and universally, no matter how we perceive those we are called to love.

By seeking to become people who are, by nature, loving, we can then share that love in a variety of ways.

Theologian John Franke asserts that, "while the mission of God is complex and multifaceted, its central character, from which all other aspects flow, is love."[1] This love, he goes on to say, is eternal for it always has been, is, and will be "because God lives eternally in the communal fellowship between Father, Son, and Holy Spirit as they participate in giving, receiving, and sharing love."[2] And this divine love is not a mere sentiment or a jealously guarded possession. This love is continually being given away through generous actions. The love of God—Father, Son, and Holy Spirit—has been expressed in creative, transformational, incarnational, liberating, and empowering ways throughout history and continues to be shared in these same ways today. You might even say that it is God's mission to give away God's love and we are called to receive and share this gift in selflessly loving ways as well. In seeking to sow love where we find hatred, I hope that we will be liberated to love as God loves and to share the liberation that love brings with those around us.

> Now the Lord is the Spirit, and where the Spirit of the
> Lord is, there is freedom. (2 Cor 3:17)

Before going any further, it seems prudent to also spend a bit of time with the word *hate*. According to Merriam-Webster, as a noun, hate is defined as "intense hostility and aversion usually deriving from fear, anger, or sense of injury." And as a verb, to hate is defined as feeling "extreme enmity toward," or "to regard with active hostility."[3] It seems, therefore, that hate is an emotion, not unlike love, that causes one to act.

Although it may be tempting to think that hate is the opposite of love, I am not certain that this is true. Some have said that

---

1. Franke, *Missional Theology*, 8.
2. Franke, *Missional Theology*, 8.
3. Merriam-Webster, "hate."

apathy or indifference is the opposite of hate while others have cited selfishness or even cynicism as love's opposite. Though these arguments are compelling, I would like to suggest that, while not the opposite of love, hate is its competitor. Love is active and so is hate. Both require a level of engagement. Just as love compels us to act on another's behalf, hate may compel us to commit a whole host of hostile actions, from using condemning or degrading language to carrying out acts of violence. Both love and hate require a level of engagement, a kind of emotional power that moves one to action. The emotions tied to hate and the actions resulting from it can only be conquered by something as powerful as agape love.

A Time for Reflection

Lord, make us instruments of your peace. Where there is hatred, let us sow love.

During the time you spend with this chapter, make a conscious effort to call this portion of the prayer to mind and offer it as a silent prayer several times each day. Incorporate it into your usual times for prayer. Call it to mind when you are waiting or engaged in other activities, like when you are at a stop light or doing the dishes or even during commercial breaks while watching TV. Meditate on it as often as possible so that it begins to shape the way you see the world around you and respond to what you see.

Set aside some time to consider your personal relationship with hate. Find a time and a place where you can be undisturbed for at least ten minutes. Use the first words of this prayer to center yourself and quiet your mind. Ask the Holy Spirit to guide your thoughts. Now, take the next few minutes to think about hate. The first time you do this, begin on a personal level. Is there anything or anyone you truly hate (not just dislike or are annoyed by)? Through the eyes of your imagination, allow the Spirit to help you form a mental picture of the person, group, system, or structure that you hate. Once you have explored that image, move on to consider where you see hate in the world around you. Obviously, none of us can know how others feel, but hate is hardly ever kept to oneself. Where have you heard or read hate speech or seen actions that were motivated by more than anger about a specific issue or person? If it helps you to write a list, do so.

Take a break, anything from a few minutes to a few days, then go back to your meditation about hate. When you remember the object of your hate, picture it once again and ask the Spirit to guide you in discerning just what about it fuels your hate. If it is a person, is there something about their actual nature or is it a behavior or behaviors that provoke such a strong reaction? If it is a group or organization or governmental body that came to mind, ask the Spirit to give you some clarity about just why its way of being in the world has moved you to hate it.

Sit with these images for a bit and then imagine how love might change them. How could love from you (or others) cause personal or institutional behaviors to change? Be specific. If you can't come up with anything that's okay. Our society has conditioned us to see that the objects of our hatred can only be defeated by the tools of hatred: an exertion of power and violence greater than that possessed by those we hate. But the Prayer of St. Francis calls us to source a different power. The power that we need to confront and defeat those things worthy of our hate is love. Take some time now to imagine how love could defeat the root of your hate. This will not be easy. It will most likely require a good deal of soul searching and imagination, so don't expect to come up with too many satisfying ideas in the next few minutes. Return to this exercise over the next few days and keep offering this challenge to God in prayer. My hope is that you will be led to a practical way of offering liberating, life-changing love to someone or some group that you hate. Obviously, this will be a difficult task. But in the words of Miyamoto Musashi, "it may seem difficult at first, but everything is difficult at first."[4]

---

4. Musashi, *Book of Five Rings*, 10. Miyamoto Musashi was a swordsman and philosopher in late sixteenth- and early seventeenth-century Japan.

Take another break. You deserve it. Now, as you go over what you have come up with, take some time in silence to consider these words from the Scriptures:

> "But I say to you that listen, Love your enemies, do good to those who hate you." (Luke 6:27)

> Those who say, "I love God," and hate their brothers or sisters, are liars; for those who do not love a brother or sister whom they have seen, cannot love God whom they have not seen. (1 John 4:20)

> Do not be overcome by evil, but overcome evil with good. (Rom 12:21)

Slowly read these passages three times. After the first reading, pause to consider what words or phrases immediately caught your attention. Following the second reading, reflect on what emotional reaction you had. And, after the third reading, ask yourself how they spoke to you about any relationship in your life or in the life of your community. Make sure that you give yourself enough time to sit with your responses to the three readings of these passages. If you find journaling a helpful spiritual discipline, record your reactions in the space below.

_____

_____

_____

_____

Did any of your reactions or responses to these Scripture passages surprise or upset you? Did this exercise open your heart and mind to some area in your life where you are experiencing hate? If so, ask yourself the following questions: How does this hate affect those I have this feeling for? Does it affect them at all? Does it limit or enslave them, preventing them from living in the fullness of God's kingdom of shalom? And how does this hatred affect me? How is it limiting or enslaving me? Spend as much time as you can with these questions. Holding a mirror to ourselves, illumed by the words of the Scriptures, can be frightening and painful, but avoiding such personal scrutiny and instead burying some of the uglier truths about ourselves cannot move us to a place of love. To help yourself explore these questions and personal confrontations honestly, you may want to note what they are in the space below. Sometimes, just writing about what we are thinking and feeling can help us to see these issues with more clarity.

_____
_____
_____
_____

End these times of reflection by offering all that you have thought and felt to God in prayer.

A Time for Action

It is time now to move your gaze away from yourself and to look outward at your community and the wider world. Take a few minutes to think about the ways you see hate being expressed in your community, the nation, and the world. Look at the news feed on your computer, skim the day's newspaper, or just log on to social media. You will probably not have to look far to find hate speech, violence, or groups or even laws that marginalize or diminish the value of individuals or groups of people.

In the space below, note those that stir up the most energy or concern within you.

_____
_____
_____
_____

Now, prayerfully consider where you have seen the Spirit working in these areas. Begin in your own congregation and denomination and move out from there. Are there individuals or groups who are challenging hate with love? How are they doing this? What actions are they taking? You will probably need to do a little research to find out about people and organizations that are battling the causes and consequences of such hate but they are there. Look for news stories that celebrate acts of kindness or generosity in the face of oppression or discrimination. You can also look for groups whose loving actions combat the consequences of hate in your area. Information about both religious and secular nonprofit groups in your area can be found through some basic sleuthing by talking to other members of your congregation who may be connected to a variety of programs and ministries. And if this is not possible you can do a simple search on Google. Try to keep your investigation focused on people and organizations whose work is specifically directed toward battling hate with love. While many good and loving activities are happening in our communities and are important ways of battling inequity (food banks, clothing drives, fundraising for the treatment of illnesses, etc.), try to limit the scope of your investigation to actions and organizations that are more clearly seeking to overcome hate with love. Note what you find in the space below.

_____

_____

_____

_____

Now it's time to take action. Remember the example of hate that stirred up the most concern and energy in you? Have you found any people, groups, or organizations who are addressing those concerns with actions based in love? If so, find a way to learn more about them and, if possible, contribute to their work. If you are unable to become physically involved, can you help in some other way, like donating money, telling others about their work, or praying for them on a regular basis? Nothing you do will be too small. Remember, you are praying to sow love where there is hate. When a farmer sows seeds, it takes time for them to germinate, grow, and produce food. But through it all the farmer tends the fields where the seed is sown by watering, weeding, and fertilizing the soil. Sowing love is no different. It begins with a small seed—a bit of money, a commitment to prayer, a change of personal behavior, an activity with others—but these actions must continue to be nurtured in order to see love grow and overcome the seeds of hate that are also being planted and tended in the same field.

What will you do to sow seeds of love where you find hate? Using the space below, note what your commitment will be and then share that information with a faithful friend who can help you remain steadfast in this commitment.

_____
_____
_____
_____

For you were called to freedom, brothers and sisters; only do not use your freedom as an opportunity for self-indulgence, but through love become slaves to one another. For the whole law is summed up in a single commandment, "You shall love your neighbor as yourself."

—GALATIANS 5:13–14

2

Where There Is Injury, Pardon

FOUNDATION

This portion of the prayer begs God to help us become healers. It pleads with God to make us into people who can fearlessly face both our own wounds and the wounds of others in an effort to forgive and reconcile. We cannot pray this lightly. We cannot pray this with the expectation that merely saying "sorry" means God will wave a magic wand and heal the hurts we have inflicted. We cannot expect a word of apology to give us the strength to immediately forgive someone who has injured us, believing that we will not have a scar from that encounter. Forgiveness is hard work. It requires the willingness to give up everything from false pride to a comforting sense of victimhood. In order to forgive others, we need to accept responsibility for the times when we have acted badly, to accept the consequences of our actions, and to make real changes in our lives. Only then is reconciliation possible. We can do none of this alone, of course, which is why we pray that God will make us instruments of God's peace who bring pardon where there is injury. We must accept God's correction and open our hearts to the power of the Holy Spirit if we are to inhabit a kingdom lifestyle that both seeks and offers forgiveness and reconciliation in our daily lives.

A Memory

> *At the beginning of the first Gulf War, some folks in the parish where I worked asked to have a special Sunday evening prayer service for peace. At that morning's regular worship service, the priest announced the event and then he said something I'd like to share.*
>
> *"All are invited to this service where prayers will be offered for peace in the Middle East. But please, don't come unless you have first made peace in your home. Before you come to beg God for an end to this conflict, be reconciled with any relative or neighbor you aren't talking to or with whom you are in conflict. Then, please, come and pray."*

I believe the Prayer of St. Francis calls us to the work of bringing pardon to places of injury in our own lives before, and then alongside, this same work in the community at large. We must be working on our own house, so to speak, to gain the skills we need before we can even offer to help build a neighborhood. By mending relationships with those who were once close to us, we will learn the almost-impossible rigor it takes to forgive and reconcile. It cannot be accomplished without God's grace. Once, by God's grace, we do forgive and reconcile with those around us, we will more clearly understand how utterly difficult it is for victims of violence, discrimination, and generational persecution to forgive and reconcile with the ones who have hurt them. If our goal is to become peacemakers who work to bring forgiveness and reconciliation to the world, we must begin with the little world that is our own heart. Therefore, we will begin with forgiveness and reconciliation at the personal level before looking at forgiveness and reconciliation in a wider context.

A Time for Reflection

Lord, make us instruments of your peace. Where there is injury, let us sow pardon.

Make a place in your daily devotions and, more importantly, throughout the day, to offer these words in prayer.

We must only pray this portion of the prayer if we are willing to allow God to remake us into people who seek reconciliation over revenge, and choose confession and amendment of life in place of a false sense of control and self-righteousness.

Self-examination can be a useful tool when beginning the journey of becoming a person who seeks to bring pardon where there has been injury.

Find a quiet and comfortable place where you can be undisturbed for ten to twenty minutes. Take a few cleansing breaths and then read the following passages from Scripture.

> Let us test and examine our ways,
>   and return to the Lord.
> Let us lift up our hearts as well as our hands
>   to God in heaven. (Lam 3:40–41)

> Examine yourselves to see whether you are living in the faith. Test yourselves. Do you not realize that Jesus Christ is in you?—unless, indeed, you fail to meet the test! (2 Cor 13:5)

With these words in mind, ask the Holy Spirit to guide you in a time of self-examination. Here are a few questions to help you get started.

In what ways have I fallen short in following Jesus?

Do I have any relationships that have been severed or injured because of something I've said or done?

Am I holding on to any old hurts or resentments that have harmed or even destroyed any relationships in my life?

If you find yourself resisting the demands of this exercise, or if this is a terribly difficult experience for you, you may want to consider the following questions before moving on.

What keeps me from looking closely at my life as a follower of Jesus to see where I am being faithful and where I have turned away? Is it fear of what I will find? Am I afraid of dredging up memories or feelings that will upset me? Do I worry that God will not forgive me?

After your time of self-examination, offer all that you have discovered to God in prayer. If you are having trouble putting all of it into words you can use the following prayer as a guide.

> Lord, thank you for loving me so completely that nothing I have done or said can separate me from you. Thank you for knowing me better than I know myself. Thank you for walking with me during this time of self-examination and helping me face the places within myself where I have turned away from you and your will for me.
>
> I confess that I have hurt others in these specific ways.

_____

_____

_____

_____

> I confess that I have held on to past hurts and have not forgiven those who have injured me.

_____

_____

_____

_____

> I have avoided confronting myself about the injuries I've inflicted and nurtured the hurts I've received, but I offer it all to you now. I am truly sorry and I humbly repent. Forgive me, Lord, and fill me with the power of your Holy

> Spirit so that I may be reconciled to those whom I've hurt and those who have hurt me. In Jesus' name I pray. Amen.

Take a moment of silence and then read the following words to remind you of God's forgiveness and the freedom that it brings.

> You were created in love and there is nothing that can separate you from that love. God—the Father who created you, the Son who redeemed you, and the Spirit who sustains you—forgives you and strengthens you to walk in newness of life. Amen.

A Time for Action

Allow some time to pass after engaging in your self-examination. Does something that came up during that exercise keep coming back to your mind? Is it something that makes you want to take some kind of action? Is there someone from whom you are estranged who keeps coming to mind? Do you feel you need to let someone (besides God) know that you are sorry for something you've done, or do you feel a growing need to share an unacknowledged hurt with someone?

You should also carefully consider why you want to reach out to someone who has wronged you. Do you want to make peace with them so that you can be in a new and right relationship or do you just want to vent about how much they hurt you? Even when dressed up with religious language, which is passive aggression at its best, this does not provide pardon for injury. So, before you write a letter or pick up the phone, ask yourself what you hope to achieve. Do you just want to be vindicated or are you willing to walk the long road of reconciliation with them so that together you can rebuild a relationship with trust and love?

Once you have prayerfully considered that your reasons for contacting those with whom you are estranged are out of love, it is time for you to act. First, think carefully about how you might want to contact the person who has been on your mind. If you are offering an apology, it is best if you can do so in person and in private.

If not, a sincere letter is a good option. If you are seeking to make peace with someone who has hurt you and they are someone you see regularly but with whom you have unresolved feelings of anger, guilt, or resentment, then a personal meeting might be best. If you are unable to meet with them in person (if they now live far away or the hurt was suffered long ago), you might want to write them a letter to carefully and lovingly express your hurt, offer forgiveness, and suggest a way of moving forward. As long as you prayerfully and lovingly approach them, there is no wrong way to do so, with one exception: it is never a good idea to use social media to post a recounting of the way you have been wronged, even if followed by an offer of forgiveness. While things like Facebook and Instagram are great ways of staying in touch with friends and acquaintances, they are not appropriate platforms for engaging in one-on-one personal requests for apologies or forgiveness. When aired in such a public arena, even small hurts and minor cracks in relationships can grow into major injuries and cavernous divisions.

If you are seeking an apology from someone whom you cannot contact because they have died or because your efforts would do more harm than good, it is probably best to write a letter that you will never send. Take your time with this exercise. Explore all your complaints and even acknowledge any responsibility you may have had for whatever happened. Go beyond the painful incident and explain how this has affected you in the time that has passed, and why you want to find a way to resolve this issue now. If you are ready and able to begin the process of forgiving this person, write about that, and if you are not there yet, explain why and describe how you are working on ways to bring yourself to forgiveness. Now, offer your letter to God in prayer, and then destroy it in a way that brings you a sense of closure—put it in a shredder, rip it up into really tiny pieces, or throw it in the fireplace. Whatever you do, use it as way to help yourself move beyond your hurt and pain so that you can be set free to offer heartfelt forgiveness.

> Happy are those whose transgression is forgiven,
>   whose sin is covered.
> Happy are those to whom the Lord imputes no iniquity,

and in whose spirit there is no deceit.
While I kept silence, my body wasted away
   through my groaning all day long.
For day and night your hand was heavy upon me;
   my strength was dried up as by the heat of summer.
Then I acknowledged my sin to you,
   and I did not hide my iniquity;
I said, "I will confess my transgressions to the Lord,"
   and you forgave the guilt of my sin.
(Ps 32:1–5)

A Time for Reflection

Forgiving and being reconciled to our enemies or our loved ones are not about pretending that things are other than they are. It is not about patting one another on the back and turning a blind eye to the wrong. True reconciliation exposes the awfulness, the abuse, the hurt, the truth. It could even sometimes make things worse. It is a risky undertaking but in the end it is worthwhile, because in the end only an honest confrontation with reality can bring real healing. Superficial reconciliation can bring only superficial healing.

—Desmond Tutu[1]

Praying for the ability to bring pardon to places of injury in our own lives is an important first step. But, as members of the body of Christ, we are also praying for the ability to extend this loving pardon well beyond our own relationships. During our time of self-reflection and work to restore right relationships in our lives, we are learning how God calls for the reconciliation of the whole world. By carefully examining and confessing our own injurious words and actions, and by offering and accepting forgiveness, we are becoming more and more sensitized to what everyone else is

---

1. Diederich, "Forgiveness Quotes."

experiencing as well. Because we have explored our own pain, we can better understand the pain of someone else. We call this empathy.

Let us now explore how our cry to bring pardon to injury can be expressed to our wider community.

The mission of God seeks reconciliation between God and humanity, between neighbors, races, cultures, and even between human beings and the rest of the created world. Through the saving grace of the death and resurrection of Jesus, God has initiated this mission by reconciling humanity to Godself. We, as the body of Christ, are now called to participate in this mission by sharing the good news of God in Christ in ways that bring about this kind of wide-reaching reconciliation as well. The kingdom of God, the kingdom of shalom, is a reconciled kingdom, not just a reconciled household or neighborhood.

Even the earliest followers of Jesus struggled with sowing pardon where there was injury. If this were not true Peter and Jesus would not have had this conversation:

> [Peter said], "Lord, if my brother or sister sins against me, how often should I forgive? As many as seven times?" Jesus said to him, "Not seven times, but I tell you, seventy-seven times." (Matt 18:22)

Members of the early church also needed to be reminded about their call to reconciliation.

> Do not repay anyone evil for evil, but take thought for what is noble in the sight of all. If it is possible, so far as it depends on you, live peaceably with all. Beloved, never avenge yourselves, but leave room for the wrath of God; for it is written, "Vengeance is mine, I will repay, says the Lord." No, "if your enemies are hungry, feed them; if they are thirsty, give them something to drink; for by doing this you will heap burning coals on their heads." Do not be overcome by evil, but overcome evil with good. (Rom 12:17–21)

And while we may think that congregational controversies that breed political rancor, incivility, and arguments over whether the pipe organ or the electric guitar is God's favorite instrument for worship are something new, we would be wrong. Members of the early church were also getting caught up in equally contentious disputes prompting Paul to pen these words:

> Have nothing to do with stupid and senseless controversies; you know that they breed quarrels. And the Lord's servant must not be quarrelsome but kindly to everyone, an apt teacher, patient, correcting opponents with gentleness. God may perhaps grant that they will repent and come to know the truth. (2 Tim 2:23–25)

Go to a quiet place where you won't be disturbed and take at least twenty to thirty minutes to prayerfully consider the three passages you've just read. As you reflect on how this call to reconciliation can be brought to bear on what you discover, ask yourself the following questions.

Questions About Your Faith Community

Does your congregation actively welcome those who are not of their predominate ethnic or socioeconomic background, or are there subtle cues that set barriers for those who are classified as "different"? In the past, did your denomination participate in mission or evangelism programs that colluded with colonialism, oppressed native cultures, or turned a blind eye to the abuse of the vulnerable? If they did, how do they approach their history now?

Questions About the Wider World

Where do you see injury in your community and the greater world? Have injustices inflicted on people in the past continued to affect their descendants today? Are there laws or policies that marginalize specific groups of people?

Questions About Your Relationship with the Natural World

How have businesses or government policies contributed to injuring the earth? How have you and your neighbors contributed to wounding the earth through the choices you make regarding what you consume or how you use natural resources?

Perhaps these are some of the injuries we should think of when we pray to be instruments of God's peace by seeking and giving pardon, and by working for reconciliation.

Take time over the next couple of days to face some of the injuries that have been inflicted within your own community. If you are having difficulty finding examples, watch a local newscast or read the morning paper.

Note the injuries you've called to mind or discovered in the space below.

_____

_____

_____

_____

In a way similar to how you've experienced Scripture through silence and reflection, read over the list you've just made, asking the Spirit to direct your thoughts to the items on your list that generated the strongest emotional response or caused you the most concern. What, if any, personal connections do you have with these manifestations of injury or pain? Do these injuries affect you or people you know? If not, prayerfully wonder why the Spirit is opening your heart to these particular people and places of hurt. When you have finished this meditation, write a list of what the Spirit brought to your attention.

_____

_____

Lord, Make Us Instruments of Your Peace

_____

_____

Now, ask the Holy Spirit to guide you in seeing the ways that people within your church, community, and/or family have been seeking or offering pardon and working toward reconciliation. Write what comes to mind in the space below.

_____

_____

_____

_____

Finally, prayerfully imagine how you might help bring pardon and reconciliation to the situations and relationships you have noted, and write those ideas in the space below.

_____

_____

_____

_____

> *To forgive is to set a prisoner free and discover that the prisoner was you.*
> —Lewis B. Smedes[2]

A Time for Action

Take a break for a few hours or a few days. Then revisit the lists you have made concerning the injuries of those within either your local community or the world at large. Now choose to get involved by participating in at least one activity that sows seeds of pardon. If you found that most of your interest was centered on the harm

---

2. AZ Quotes, "Lewis B. Smedes."

that has been done to the earth, commit to getting involved with a project that works to heal the injuries that have been committed. If you are unable to connect with one such group you can at least grab some gloves and a garbage bag to clean up plastic and other waste that would otherwise end up in the waters of lakes, rivers, or oceans.

If racism is the wound that causes you the most concern, check out your denomination's website to see if there are programs within your church that are working to sow seeds of healing in places that have been injured by historical and continuing racism. You can also visit the National League of Cities website to read an article about how the old policy of redlining continues to affect communities of color in cities all over this country.[3] This article was written by Terrance L. Hamm, a communications specialist for the Institute for Youth, Education, and Families, and the Center for Race, Equity, and Leadership. The site also provides ideas and resources for getting involved in healing activities.

The best way to combat feelings of despair due to the many people and places that have been injured by past and continuing human behavior is to get involved in the healing process. You just may need to do a little research to find out where your concerns and gifts can be best used in your particular community.

Forgiveness does not mean ignoring what has been done or putting a false label on an evil act. It means, rather, that the evil act no longer remains as a barrier to the relationship. Forgiveness is a catalyst creating the atmosphere necessary for a fresh start and a new beginning.

—Martin Luther King Jr.[4]

---

3. Hamm, "Reversing the Residual Effects"
4. King, *Gift of Love*, 65.

OPTIONAL ACTIVITY

Invite a group of friends to join you in watching the 2020 movie *Burden*. If possible, host a viewing party followed by a discussion. Based on a true story, this movie is set in a southern community scarred from deep-rooted racism and tells the story of the unlikely friendship that forms when an African American pastor helps a KKK member leave the Klan. He offers pardon for the injuries this man has caused and then leads his fellow Christians into a place where they too can forgive and enter into a relationship with the former Klansman. You can rent *Burden* on streaming services like Amazon Prime or YouTube. (Please note: This film is rated R because of violence and rough language but at its heart it is all about the redeeming love of God.)[5]

---

5. To check out the trailer, visit the link in the bibliography under 101 Studios.

3

Where There Is Discord, Union

FOUNDATION

In this portion of the prayer, we pray to sow seeds that will grow in unity rather than discord. But what are we really praying for? We must tread carefully. The word *unity* can be misidentified as uniformity. It can be misconstrued and used in ways that support our own selfish desires. What we are praying for is a kind of unity that does not diminish the value of each unique individual.

I was not someone who was blessed with great musical ability. I can sing the hymns in church if I am standing next to someone who is singing on pitch and loudly enough for me to parrot. Harmony, however, escapes me. If everyone were like me music would be very boring indeed. Imagine an orchestra made up of only one type of instrument all playing only the melody. That is musical uniformity. Musical unity is much more dynamic and interesting. For example, in a choir a diversity of voices are singing a variety of parts, each different, but each adding to the larger piece of music. An orchestra features a wide variety of instruments, each with a unique timbre, playing varied parts of the same piece of music. There is not just melody and harmony but counterpoints and rhythmic undercurrents as well. The conductor keeps the unity in place while allowing each individual part to contribute to the whole in its own unique way.

Like the musicians in the orchestra, members of the church community are called to this same kind of diversified unity. Unfortunately, many church communities fall prey to fear and the desire for control and power. They end up seeking uniformity over unity, fealty over expression. What looks like unity can actually be oppression. This, obviously, is not the kind of union for which we pray. Neither do we pray for everyone (even our children) to always agree with our beliefs, values, or rules in the name of harmony and peace. On the contrary, when we pray for the ability to bring union into times of discord, we are praying to have our own eyes opened and our hearts expanded. We are praying to seek unity within difference, to accept and encourage, and to find common ground with those who differ from us in any number of ways. And we do this with one goal in mind: to welcome others in sharing the love of God in Christ as we boldly step into a kingdom of shalom lifestyle.

When we pray for empowerment to confront discord by sowing seeds of union, we are praying for the ability to acknowledge and celebrate the diversity of God's creation rather than responding with suspicion or resistance to those whose opinions or traditions are different from our own.

God created the world with a diversity of life forms, each with its own unique beauty and purpose. The Prayer of St. Francis reminds us that we are to embrace that diversity by sowing seeds of appreciation and acceptance in places where our differences have caused discord, so that we might find union with one another, not in spite of our differences, but because of them.

A Time for Reflection

Lord, make us instruments of your peace. Where there is discord, let us sow union.

Prayerfully read the following passage from Romans.

WHERE THERE IS DISCORD, UNION

> For by the grace given to me I say to everyone among you not to think of yourself more highly than you ought to think, but to think with sober judgment, each according to the measure of faith that God has assigned. For as in one body we have many members, and not all the members have the same function, so we, who are many, are one body in Christ, and individually we are members one of another. (Rom 12:3–5)

After spending some time with these words, spend some time reflecting on your place or role in the body of Christ. Make a quick list of your specific gifts you can use to serve as a member of Christ's body. Don't limit yourself to thinking about how you can serve during times of worship or only within the confines of your church community. Think about how you are using or can use your gifts as an expression of your relationship with Jesus and his body in your everyday life.

_____

_____

_____

_____

Read the passage again and ask yourself how your gifts and the way you use them are supported or encouraged by the gifts of others. Are there ways that you feel called to love and serve that would not be possible without the help of those with different gifts? Make a note of what you discover in the space below.

_____

_____

_____

_____

Read the passage one more time and then broaden your view to consider what your local arm of the body of Christ (your congregation) looks like. Who are in positions of leadership? Who serves in ministries within the parish (e.g., helping with administrative tasks; serving during worship as leaders, choir members, ushers, etc.; teaching; mentoring and encouraging; cleaning and fixing; cooking and childcare)? Challenge yourself to think about all the roles your brothers and sisters play within the life of your faith community. What about the people you don't see participating in visible ways? Could they have personal ministries of intercessory prayer? Do they routinely call and visit those who are ill or alone? Try to imagine the many ways that the members of your congregation are contributing to the union you call your church and sharing the church's love with the greater world. If you were to make a list of all that you discovered during this time of wondering, you would probably be amazed at how long and varied it would be. Continuing with this journey of the imagination, now think about what the members of your community do outside of the church and its ministries. Are there parents (and grandparents) lovingly raising children? Do any work in jobs that serve the public good? Do some help out at homeless shelters or food banks while others participate in protests against injustice? Do any teach or mentor youth?

Take some time over the next few days to pray for the various members of your community who have come to mind during this exercise. Give thanks for them and ask the Holy Spirit to help you to continue to discern the ways in which you can use your gifts in ways that support and harmonize with the gifts of others.

A Time for Action

The Christians in Corinth needed to be reminded of the beauty of diversity within unity, and so do we.

> For just as the body is one and has many members, and all the members of the body, though many, are one body, so it is with Christ. For in the one Spirit we were all baptized into one body—Jews or Greeks, slaves or free—and we were all made to drink of one Spirit.

> Indeed, the body does not consist of one member but of many. If the foot would say, "Because I am not a hand, I do not belong to the body," that would not make it any less a part of the body. And if the ear would say, "Because I am not an eye, I do not belong to the body," that would not make it any less a part of the body. If the whole body were an eye, where would the hearing be? If the whole body were hearing, where would the sense of smell be? But as it is, God arranged the members in the body, each one of them, as he chose. If all were a single member, where would the body be? As it is, there are many members, yet one body. The eye cannot say to the hand, "I have no need of you," nor again the head to the feet, "I have no need of you." On the contrary, the members of the body that seem to be weaker are indispensable, and those members of the body that we think less honorable we clothe with greater honor, and our less respectable members are treated with greater respect; whereas our more respectable members do not need this. But God has so arranged the body, giving the greater honor to the inferior member, that there may be no dissension within the body, but the members may have the same care for one another. If one member suffers, all suffer together with it; if one member is honored, all rejoice together with it.
>
> Now you are the body of Christ and individually members of it. (1 Cor 12:12–27)

If, during your time of prayerful reflection, you found that you didn't know much about the way in which your fellow Christ followers are sharing God's love in their everyday lives, then take the time to find out. Read the monthly and weekly announcements about the ministries in your church and the ministries that your church sponsors outside its walls. Chat with people at coffee hour. Be nosey. I think you will be surprised by the way the Spirit is already moving in the lives of your fellow churchgoers and even more surprised by the diversity of gifts you will find as well as the variety of ways those gifts are being shared. Once you have learned more about the gifts of your fellow Christ followers, make note of what surprised or inspired you the most in the space below.

_____

_____

_____

_____

A Memory

When I was in my twenties, I used to roll my eyes as I watched one member of the Altar Guild go about her duties. She was painstakingly fastidious and routinely took at least twice as much time as anyone else to lay out the linens or set up the chalice and paten before the worship service. Once, between the two morning services, I saw her drag an ironing board into the sanctuary in order to iron the ends of the cloth that stretched over the altar and hung down over two of its sides. Unable to hold my opinions to myself I made a (snarky) joke.

Rather than reacting in anger (or even just ignoring me) she stopped, looked at me, and quietly said. "The Eucharist is the most important part of the worship service and I don't want anything I've done (even leaving wrinkles in this cloth) to distract people from focusing on that."

After so beautifully being put in my place, I developed a whole new appreciation for the service of others—no matter what it was or how it was offered.

Be honest, do you value the work done by some of your fellow parishioners more than others? Do you think of the person who can teach or preach as being more important than the one who sets up and puts away tables and chairs for congregational events? Does the old man in the wheelchair who greets each child with a smile as they enter the church building seem less vital to the life of the church than the woman who organizes the outreach events? What would your community life look like without these and other people who serve, not as public faces, but as quiet helpers or encouragers? Make a list of at least five people in your congregation who serve in essential but mostly invisible ways. The members on your list can range from anyone who routinely prays for the congregation on the weekly list of intercessions to those who pick up litter on the church grounds or clean up after coffee hour.

_____
_____
_____
_____

Choose at least one of the people on your list and write them a note of thanks for their service.

> In the midst of a world torn asunder by discord, God calls people to tell a different story and live an alternative life, a life in which the social conventions that divide people from each other—race, ethnicity, gender, social/economic class, sexual orientation, political preferences, ideologies, and any other construction that human beings can invent to suggest that some people are inferior and unworthy of God's blessing—are set aside for a vision of unity in the midst of diversity and difference. One faith is expressed in many voices committed to unity for the sake of the world.[1]

Read 1 Cor 12:12–27 one more time.

How does this image of the body of Christ relate to your experience with your congregation, with your denomination, with the church as the body of all believers? Do you see this image being lived out or ignored? Has hierarchy and a capitulation to the secular notions of achievement and success invaded the church of your experience? Reflecting on this passage from 1 Corinthians, and the quote above, prayerfully consider how you can seek unity in diversity and value all people equally. In the space below, write at least three specific ways in which you are being called to seek and work for this kind of unity.

1. Soerens, *Everywhere You Look*, 142.

Lord, Make Us Instruments of Your Peace

_____
_____
_____
_____

Share your list with a faithful friend and then commit to finding a way to act on at least one of your responses in the week ahead. Also, ask your friend to hold you accountable for doing so.

Unity is achieved when we see the imago Dei in one another, when we refuse to live by the cultural script that some lives have more value than others. Unity thus honors diversity. Unity requires vigilant curiosity, a common story, and the kind of humility that most of us (me included) do not value.

—Tim Soerens[2]

*How very good and pleasant it is
when kindred live together in unity!*

—Psalm 133:1

---

2. Soerens, *Everywhere You Look*, 88.

4

Where There Is Doubt, Faith

FOUNDATION

What does faith mean to you? The author of the Letter to the Hebrews says that "faith is the assurance of things hoped for, the conviction of things not seen" (Heb 11:1). But how do we find that assurance or share that kind of conviction? Are we called merely to accept and then instruct others in the creeds and confessions of our particular branch of the Christian faith? Have we failed in sowing faith where there is doubt if the doubter cannot assent to a particular set of assertions or pray a specific prayer? What do you think?

Christian faith, as defined by theologian Bryan Stone, is "a matter of 'loyalty' to Christ rather than the blind acceptance of doctrine."[1] And this loyalty means following in the way of Jesus by "loving God with all your heart, and with all your soul, and with all your strength, and with all your mind; and your neighbor as yourself" (Luke 10:27).

Over the centuries, faith has often been taken to mean an intellectual assent to a set of beliefs, but for the earliest followers of Jesus, faith was participatory. Having been transformed through the grace of baptism, the faithful were empowered to walk in the way of faith.

---

1. Stone, *Evangelism After Christendom*, 154.

> Therefore, we have been buried with him by baptism into death, so that, just as Christ was raised from the dead by the glory of the Father, so we too might walk in newness of life. (Rom 6:4)

Because God is faithful in God's missional love for all of creation, we, the created, are also called into a life of faithfulness in fellowship with Jesus the ascended and living Lord.

> God is faithful; by him you were called into the fellowship of his Son, Jesus Christ our Lord. (1 Cor 1:9)

So, what does this mean for those of us who cry out to the Lord, "Make us instruments of your peace: where there is doubt, let us sow faith"?

Doubt, by itself, is not such a bad thing. A little self-doubt can save us from an arrogant belief in our own self-sufficiency. Doubt is also not necessarily a negative certainty that rejects any and all aspects of faith. Instead, honest doubt, healthy doubt, provides space for unknowing as well as the desire to fill that space by posing questions that pursue some form of knowledge. Doubt can be a good starting point, a fertile ground into which we can plant seeds of faith.

In his book *Reaching for the Invisible God*, Philip Yancey writes of doubt in the following way:

> Doubt is the skeleton in the closet of faith, and I know no better way to treat a skeleton than to bring it into the open and expose it for what it is: not something to hide or fear, but a hard structure on which living tissue may grow.[2]

When we pray to sow seeds of faith in places of doubt, we are not asking to be given specific answers that will shut down further inquiry. We are praying for two specific gifts. We are praying for the gift of faith for ourselves—faith that we are who God created us to be, that God's will and God's love will triumph in the end, and that we can always depend on God's love. This is not a one-time petition, for we will encounter circumstances and struggles that will test that

---

2. Yancey, *Reaching for the Invisible God*, 41.

faith. This is why we continue to pray for faith throughout our lives. And, at the same time, we are praying for the patience of a farmer so that we can plant seeds of faith to grow in others—while still respecting and caring for the soil of doubt that surrounds them—in the hope that those seeds germinate and grow.

Another sort of doubt, apart from the healthy doubt that encourages learning, can spring from fear, anger and angst. It is often expressed as doubt in God's sovereignty, God's love, or both. It is an understandable doubt. People who turn to this kind of doubt are often also experiencing suffering and pain. When people are subjected to unspeakable trauma or devastating loss, when they are confronted with the seeming meaninglessness of tragedy, they can entertain, even embrace, doubt and disbelief—doubt even in the existence of a loving God. Whereas the first type of doubt I described came from the head, the doubt I'm talking about here comes from the heart. Perhaps you've experienced this kind of doubt as a result of suffering or know someone who has. This kind of doubt is not necessarily unhealthy and can, at times, be beneficial as it can cause us to look more deeply into our ideas about God and God's relationship with us. Whatever the case, times of loss and suffering are times when we are most called to plant the seeds of faith in loving and patient ways. When we are hurting and fearing that God has abandoned us or is not even there at all, we should allow ourselves to lament, grieve, and even express our anger at God. We are in relationship with God after all, and this is all part of the ongoing dialogue that takes place between the two of us throughout our lives. We are reminded of this by the laments and pleas we find in the words of prophets and psalmists alike. It is also important to be patient with ourselves during such difficult times while being open to the patient grace of God. We are called to this kind of loving patience when other people are hurting as well. We cry out with this part of the prayer, not so we can convince them that they are wrong to doubt, but so we can have the faith to love them, to walk beside them, and to live out of our own belief that, despite all signs and circumstances to the contrary,

> neither death, nor life, nor angels, nor rulers, nor things present, nor things to come, nor powers, nor height, nor depth, nor anything else in all creation, will be able to separate us from the love of God in Christ Jesus our Lord. (Rom 8:38–39)

To pray for faith in place of doubt then, is to pray to be empowered to face our own doubts, and the doubts of others, with openness and love; to ask questions and to be patient when answers do not come quickly or at all.

> "Teacher, I brought you my son; he has a spirit that makes him unable to speak; and whenever it seizes him, it dashes him down; and he foams and grinds his teeth and becomes rigid." . . . When the spirit saw [Jesus], immediately it convulsed the boy, and he fell on the ground and rolled about, foaming at the mouth. Jesus asked the father, "How long has this been happening to him?" And he said, "From childhood. It has often cast him into the fire and into the water, to destroy him; but if you are able to do anything, have pity on us and help us." Jesus said to him, "If you are able!—All things can be done for the one who believes." Immediately the father of the child cried out, "I believe; help my unbelief!" (Mark 9:17–24)

In this portion of the Prayer of St. Francis we, like the father who sought healing for his son, cry out to God: "I believe; help my unbelief!"

A Time for Reflection

Lord, make us instruments of your peace. Where there is doubt, let us sow faith.

Remember to be faithful in calling to mind this portion of the prayer as often as possible during the days ahead. Find a quiet place where you won't be disturbed, and prayerfully read the following passage from Scripture.

> Now faith is the assurance of things hoped for, the conviction of things not seen.... By faith we understand that the worlds were prepared by the word of God, so that what is seen was made from things that are not visible. (Heb 11:1, 3)

As you read it the first time, note what words or phrases catch your attention. Sit with those for a bit, wonder about them, argue with them.

Read this passage a second time, and consider "unseen" things, both unseen things you have questions about and the unseen things you take on faith. (While introducing the topic of the Holy Spirit I once challenged a class of seventh graders to tell me if they knew of something that was real but could never be seen. I had no idea what they would come up with. Within a few moments one of them said "time." Yes, God's missional love is creative, and we are called to be creative too.)

Now, as you read this passage one last time, consider what you hope for. This kind of hope is not synonymous with wishing. I may wish I had a prehensile tail but I live in hope for the day that "every knee shall bend and every tongue confess that Jesus Christ is Lord" (Phil 2:11). Hopes are expectations grounded in trust while wishes are desires for some thing or outcome we want.

In the space below, make a note of the feelings, questions, answers, and hopes that this passage provoked in you.

_____
_____
_____
_____

> *The strength of your faith is not measured by the absence of doubt, but by the faithfulness of your life in the face of doubt.*
> —Nicky Gumbel[3]

---

3. Gumbel, "Strength of Your Faith."

Take a break. Put these considerations away until another time. When you return to your quiet place, take some time to think about the disciple Thomas.

Much has been written about Thomas and his doubts.

> "Unless I see the mark of the nails in his hands, and put my finger in the mark of the nails and my hand in his side, I will not believe." (John 20:25)

But this is the same Thomas who had, not so many days before this, when the other disciples were trying to dissuade Jesus from going to Judea ("Rabbi, the Jews were just now trying to stone you, and are you going there again?"), said "Let us also go, that we may die with him" (John 11:8,16). This man's faith in Jesus was so great that he was willing to die for and with him. And yet, for centuries, he has been called "doubting Thomas." Didn't other disciples doubt the words of the women who had first brought them news of the risen Lord? (Luke 24:10–11). Maybe Thomas was just bringing his skeleton of doubt out of the closet in hopes that Jesus himself would replace it with his own resurrected body.

Prayerfully read this passage from the Gospel of John.

> But Thomas (who was called the Twin), one of the twelve, was not with them when Jesus came. So the other disciples told him, "We have seen the Lord." But he said to them, "Unless I see the mark of the nails in his hands, and put my finger in the mark of the nails and my hand in his side, I will not believe." (John 20:24–25)

As you read it the first time, try to imagine the scene when Thomas is told that the others have seen the risen Lord. How do they share this information? Are they excited, all talking at once? Or are they still in a state of awe and having difficulty explaining what this experience was like?

Now, read it again and imagine that you are Thomas. What thoughts or feelings are you experiencing? Are you angry that you missed this big event, do you feel hurt at being left out, or are you just doubtful that it happened at all? These are people you have spent a great deal of time with. You've shared some amazing experiences with them because of Jesus. Why do you doubt what they are saying now?

Try to imagine what the week after this initial event was like for Thomas and the others. Was there tension between them? Did one or more of them try to convince Thomas that they had really seen the risen Lord? Did Thomas feel somehow estranged from the "true believers" in the group? Thomas confessed his doubts, yet he did not leave the community of believers. Take some time to wonder why. Did the behavior of the others toward him have anything to do with him sticking around?

Now, read the next part of the story.

> A week later his disciples were again in the house, and Thomas was with them. Although the doors were shut, Jesus came and stood among them and said, "Peace be with you." Then he said to Thomas, "Put your finger here and see my hands. Reach out your hand and put it in my side. Do not doubt but believe." Thomas answered him, "My Lord and my God!" Jesus said to him, "Have you believed because you have seen me? Blessed are those who have not seen and yet have come to believe." (John 20:26–29)

Imagine Jesus approaching Thomas. What are the other disciples doing? Imagine yourself as Thomas. How are you feeling? What are you thinking?

Spend as much time as you can just imagining this scene and wondering about all of those who were present. To close, give thanks to God that, even during your times of doubt, you are one of the blessed who have not seen and yet believe.

A Time for Action

When we pray to sow seeds of faith in places where there is doubt we assume that we are talking about faith in God: Father, Son, and Holy Spirit. But some people cannot even begin to claim such faith because their experiences—childhood abuse, failures in relationships or jobs, etc.—have left them unable to put faith in anything or anyone, including themselves. Perhaps this is where we need to begin planting seeds of faith.

Do you know someone who is going through a difficult time? Perhaps a loved one has died or they've lost their job, their teenager has gotten into trouble, or their spouse has asked for a divorce. Modern life has no shortages of challenges. These challenges cause many to lose faith in themselves, other people, institutions, and even God. How can you be the kind of farmer friend they need so that seeds of faith can grow (or grow again) in their lives? Being faithful in your friendship is the first step, I think. Before planting seeds, farmers must first prepare the soil so that it has the right mix of nutrients, the appropriate aeration, and a ready supply of water before any seeds are sown. This is what steadfast friendship can do for someone for whom faith is a struggle.

Prayerfully consider who, in your extended family, your faith community, or your circle of friends might be experiencing a time of challenge right now. Are they down on themselves, have they given up trying to get a job or help with a problem from businesses and agencies that have disappointed them? Have they left the church? Identify one person from those who come to mind whom you feel called to faithfully pray for and walk with.

Begin with prayer. Ask for the opportunities, the appropriate words, and actions you'll need to reach out to this person. Then, just spend some time with them. If they are not close by or can't have in-person visits because of health issues, reach out by phone, text, or email. Use whatever method seems most accessible for them. Walking with them and listening, without giving advice or proselytizing, is one way to prepare their hearts to receive the seeds of faith that the Holy Spirit will plant within them. You may have to listen to the same story (or complaint) time and time again, and to respond with words like, "this really is a difficult/painful/sad time for you," or "How can I pray for you?" etc. Pray for them often and remind them in gentle ways that you are doing so. Celebrate even small victories with them and encourage them; don't promise happy endings or quote scriptures in a prescriptive way. Listen.

Love. Pray. And most of all, have faith that God is working in them and through you to plant those seeds of faith.

A Memory

> *Once, when I was living in Rwanda, I was with a group of missionaries who were gathered to celebrate with a couple who had just had a baby. This was the culmination of a long journey for this couple. They had struggled with infertility and suffered a miscarriage, so the birth of this healthy baby was one that brought a special sense of joy. At one point the new mother addressed the group. She acknowledged the heartache that had preceded this happy day and then said, "Thank you for keeping us in your prayers during this long journey. And thank you most of all for having faith when we were unable to have faith ourselves. Your faith kept us going."*

This is how the seeds of faith are most often planted, not by the best or most persuasive sermon or through the words of a dynamic evangelist or author, but by everyday people like you and me being faithful intercessors and friends. And by accepting the faithful prayers and friendship of others when we are experiencing times of doubt.

Being faithful, having faith, and walking with those who have yet to discover or who have lost their faith is a gift. It takes time and, like love, this kind of faith "bears all things, believes all things, hopes all things, endures all things" (1 Cor 13:7).

How can you walk in faith with someone you know in the coming weeks and months?

It is not as a child that I believe and confess Jesus Christ. My hosanna is born of a furnace of doubt.

—FYODOR DOSTOEVSKY[4]

---

4. Conway, *Doubting Toward Faith*, 13.

5

Where There Is Despair, Hope

FOUNDATION

Despair is not merely a state of unhappiness or deep sadness caused by loss or pain. Despair is the complete loss or absence of hope. A person in a state of despair cannot imagine any possibility for a solution to their state or even a bit of relief from it. Despair creates a barrier that keeps us from seeing anything beyond the situation we find ourselves in. It prevents us from imagining an end to our present pain. Just as a person lost in the woods might well give up on trying to find their way home, lie down, go to sleep, and surrender their life to the wilderness, a person in despair may give up seeking help from other people and even cease to pray because their despair has blinded them to any possibility of being saved. Praying to be able to hope is actually praying for the powerful fist of God's love to knock down the walls that despair has built and set free those who have been imprisoned by them.

Despair cripples our ability to imagine and even think about a time or circumstance that is different from the one we feel imprisoned by. Hope offers us the opportunity to envision a time when the circumstances of our lives can be different and the feelings that oppress us can be banished.

WHERE THERE IS DESPAIR, HOPE

When we pray for hope in the midst of despair, we are not asking for a magic wand to make all our problems, griefs, and fears immediately disappear. That kind of prayer is wishful thinking—the desire for things to work out the way we want them to. Wishful thinking centers our focus around ourselves and what can be immediately satisfying to us. But hope centers our focus around God. When we pray for hope we are praying that God will give us a new perspective, that God will grant us the ability to see beyond our present circumstances. We are praying for the ability to recognize that God's loving presence is with us at this very moment, in every breath we take, no matter what is happening around us.

In his book *Looking for God in Messy Places: A Book About Hope*, Jake Owensby offers a clear distinction between hope and what people often call hope but that is, in reality, wishful thinking.

> The problem arises when getting what we want becomes our reason for living and we enlist God as the guarantor of our desired future. Again, this is wishful thinking. Hope, much more than wishful thinking, gives us the power to persevere and the stamina to endure.[1]

Hope helps us face whatever life has in store for us because hope, unlike wishful thinking, is grounded in the knowledge of God's abiding and eternal love. It is through this love that we come to know who we are and whose we are: we were created and are held in God's love. We matter, our lives have purpose. We are loved and we can share that love. When in despair we believe the opposite—that we do not matter, that there is no reason for us to endure or even live. But hope says "that life is worth living because love dwells within us and pours out from us—a love that has the power to make life worth living."[2]

Nevertheless, even the most faithful among us can fall into times of despair:

---

1. Owensby, *Looking for God*, 5.
2. Owensby, *Looking for God*, 14.

Lord, Make Us Instruments of Your Peace

> Insults have broken my heart, so that I am in despair. I looked for pity, but there was none; and for comforters, but I found none. (Ps 69:20)

Have you ever, like the psalmist, been lost in despair? Have you ever felt that there was no comfort that could possibly ease your pain? Many people experience times of despair when nothing that anyone can say or do relieves their suffering. How could we possibly bring hope to times like this in our own lives or offer hope to someone else who is enduring such anguish? I'm not sure that we can—at least not on our own. Trite sayings like "this too will pass" or "life gets better" may be well-intentioned but they do not offer any kind of real hope.

Fortunately, "we have our hope set on the living God, who is the Savior of all people, especially of those who believe" (1 Tim 4:10). Of course, just quoting this or any other Bible verse is not going to be any more helpful than the aforementioned secular sayings. But when we remind ourselves that our God is the God who set the people of Israel free from enslavement in the power-rich and militarily strong nation of Egypt, that our God is the God who delivered Jesus from death to a new life that continues for eternity, we are encouraged to breathe hope into our own desperate situations and offer that hope to others as well. In both of these examples (and many, many more) God reverses an irreversible situation, changing *what is*, to *what can be*. God does this by being present to those who are in despair. When the Israelites were being broken under the wheel of slavery, God called Moses to give them hope by reminding them that God had not abandoned them. God was, in fact, in the midst of them. Likewise, when Jesus died in a public and humiliating way, the disciples plunged into despair. But God came to them in person. The risen Lord appeared to them, spoke with them, comforted them, and instructed them on a number of occasions.

The stories of the Israelites' deliverance from slavery to freedom and Jesus' deliverance from death to eternal life can help guide us toward an answer to this portion of our prayer. But we are not guided by what happened at the end of those stories—the rescue from Egypt and the resurrection of Jesus—as much as we are by what happened before those triumphs: when God's people were in despair, God showed up and kindled hope. God was always there, always loving even during the bleakest days. Hope came when the people realized that God had not abandoned them. God was present. When we encounter those who have been moved to a place of despair, we need to be present too. In showing up, we are able to share the incarnational love of God with those we walk beside.

Be especially vigilant in keeping this portion of the prayer in your heart and mind throughout the coming days.

A Time for Reflection

Lord, make us instruments of your peace. Where there is despair, let us sow hope.

Find a quiet place where you can be undisturbed and set aside at least thirty minutes for this prayerful experience with memory and healing. Settle yourself, and read this passage from Lamentations.

> I have forgotten what happiness is;
> so I say, "Gone is my glory,
>   and all that I had hoped for from the Lord."
> The thought of my affliction and my homelessness
>   is wormwood and gall!
> My soul continually thinks of it
>   and is bowed down within me.
> (Lam 3:17–20)

As you read and reread these words, call to mind a time when you were in despair. Immerse yourself in this memory. Remember where you were, what your surroundings were like, your thoughts and feelings at the time. This will be painful, but sit with this memory until you have recreated the situation and your response to it as fully as possible. Now, clear your mind and slowly repeat the end of this passage several times.

> But this I call to mind,
>   and therefore I have hope:

> The steadfast love of the Lord never ceases,
>   his mercies never come to an end;
> they are new every morning;
>   great is your faithfulness.
> "The Lord is my portion," says my soul,
>   "therefore I will hope in him." (Lam 3:21–24)

After spending time with these words of hope, return to your memory, only this time invite our risen Savior to join you. Imagine Jesus walking through this difficult time with you. Stay close to him and allow his presence to give you strength, peace, and, especially, hope.

Take a break for a few hours or a few days and then return to your prayerful consideration of what it means to sow hope in place of despair. What have you discovered about hope? Have you found it to be more of a perspective about life and less about the specific circumstances you live in and through? Or have you discovered something else entirely? Make note of what you've learned in the space below.

_____
_____
_____
_____

A Time for Action

Gather with a few faithful friends and prayerfully discuss together what being in despair looks like. (Anyone who has ever suffered from clinical depression will be fluent in the language of despair but so will those who have lived through great loss or trauma.) Do you find evidence of despair in your community? Are there certain neighborhoods where poverty or crime has taken hold and those who live there seem to have given up on even imagining solutions to these problems? Do you think that these people in these places may feel invisible or like they don't matter to the rest of society?

Are certain problems in your town or city just accepted now because no one—from elected officials to community organizations to individual citizens—can imagine anything better than what is? Some such problems could involve the issues of homelessness, addiction, or climate change. Do you, too, feel despair when you think about any of these concerns?

If so, how can you work together to plant seeds of hope (even among yourselves) when you encounter such places and situations of despair? Try this: take some time to look for signs of hope that are already present (but perhaps not so visible) in at least one of the areas you've identified. Ask each member of the group to find a person or group who is being present for someone who is experiencing despair. These are the people who are sowing seeds of hope in places of despair.

You can also search for ministries or programs within your congregation or denomination that are planting seeds of hope by offering gifts or services that help bring change. See if there are other churches and religious organizations involved in this way. Research the service clubs and nonprofit organizations active in your community along with any government programs that are addressing your area of concern. How are they showing up? How are they sharing God's love by abiding with those in need? How are they offering hope?

After taking the time to do this research, get back together and discuss your findings. Does at least one of the ministries or agencies you've discovered spark hope within you? If so, commit together to getting involved with that group.

You can also ask your group of faithful friends if any of them knows of someone who is enduring a time of despair. Ask if any of them can identify an individual or family whose despair has led to isolation or an overriding sense of inertia. If any names come up during this time, commit to praying for them. Pray that the Spirit will lead your group to discover ways that each of you might be able to be present with those in despair. After a few days, touch base with those who have made these commitments to pray. Has anyone been inspired to any particular kind of action? Who knows where the Spirit will lead you? You may be led to pay friendly visits to someone who has walled themselves off from others because of their feelings of hopelessness. Maybe you'll feel called to sit with someone in the hospital or do some chores for a caregiver who is overwhelmed. Whatever happens and however you act, make note of it in the space below.

_____

_____

_____

_____

After a few weeks, regather with your friends to discuss and pray about your experiences in working to sow seeds of hope in despairing hearts. Talk about the ways that this may have encouraged you to do more of this kind of work and how you may have experienced hope through this exercise.

> For you are my hope, Lord GOD, my security since I was young. I depended on you since birth, when you brought me from my mother's womb; I praise you continuously. (Ps 71:5–6)

May your choices reflect your hopes, not your fears.

—NELSON MANDELA[3]

---

3. Mandela, *Long Walk to Freedom*, 174.

6

Where There Is Darkness, Light

[Jesus said] "I am the light of the world. Whoever follows me will never walk in darkness but will have the light of life."

—John 8:12

For it is the God who said, "Let light shine out of darkness," who has shone in our hearts to give the light of the knowledge of the glory of God in the face of Jesus Christ.

—2 Corinthians 4:6

FOUNDATION

Darkness can be experienced in many ways. Physical darkness can prevent us from seeing both the dangers and the opportunities that may be right in front of us. Psychological or emotional darkness can keep us from understanding either the help or harm that our thoughts and actions can cause. Spiritual darkness can lead to despair. And the darkness of ignorance can keep us from making sound decisions that can affect our own lives and the lives of others.

Lord, Make Us Instruments of Your Peace

> It is you who light my lamp; the Lord, my God, lights up my darkness. (Ps 18:28)

For the purposes of this study, I am limiting our focus to the darkness of ignorance, but I am not using the word in a pejorative sense. Rather, I am using it to mean the lack of accurate information. Without accurate information about a given situation, we cannot make sound decisions because we are unable to see and thus understand what exactly we are facing. If we were lost in the woods on starless night and without a flashlight, we would not be able to find a path or avoid dangers or even patches of poison ivy. Trying to find our way in the darkness would be futile at best. Our only recourse would be to stay alert until sunrise.

In the same way that a flashlight can carve a safe pathway through a dark place, knowledge and understanding can illuminate possibilities within seemingly impossible situations. And that kind of light—a light that brings knowledge, and more importantly, wisdom—is yet another gift from our loving God.

> O send out your light and your truth; let them lead me;
> let them bring me to your holy hill and to your dwelling.
> (Ps 43:3)

Unfortunately, darkness is still present in this world. Many people in our communities today find themselves in dark places. They can't see a way out of the circumstances that trap them in homelessness, poverty, or abusive relationships, etc. Perhaps because we have volunteered for, given money to, or even just seen a presentation about some of the resources available to people in need, we wonder why more people aren't taking advantage of the help being offered to them. Perhaps we wonder about this because we too are in the dark. If we really want to sow seeds of light in places of darkness, if our desire is to follow the Holy Spirit into our communities to share the good news of Christ by shining light in the darkness, then our journey must first begin by praying for the light of understanding within ourselves.

A Time for Reflection

Lord, make us instruments of your peace. Where there is darkness, let us sow light.

Before going any further, call to mind this part of the prayer and keep it in your heart and mind throughout the next week.

Find a quiet place where you won't be disturbed and spend some time prayerfully considering these words from the first letter of John.

> This is the message we have heard from him and proclaim to you, that God is light and in him there is no darkness at all. If we say that we have fellowship with him while we are walking in darkness, we lie and do not do what is true; but if we walk in the light as he himself is in the light, we have fellowship with one another, and the blood of Jesus his Son cleanses us from all sin. If we say that we have no sin, we deceive ourselves, and the truth is not in us. If we confess our sins, he who is faithful and just will forgive us our sins and cleanse us from all unrighteousness. If we say that we have not sinned, we make him a liar, and his word is not in us. (1 John 1:5–10)

What words or phrases leap out at you as you read this passage?

Read the passage again while asking the Spirit to help you identify areas of darkness within yourself. Do you only listen to news from one source and only discuss issues with people who agree with you? Do you feel animosity about any person or group of persons that you really don't know much about? Is there an uncomfortable truth about yourself that you purposely keep from examining in times of prayer? Don't rush this time of self-examination. Be brave. Dig deep.

Read these words from John one last time and then ask for the light of Christ to illumine any thoughts and feelings you may have that are based on little or no real knowledge. For example: are you angry at a neighbor who has allowed his yard to go uncared-for or his house to fall into disrepair? Do you just assume he is lazy or cheap? Maybe he is, or maybe he is ill or has lost his job or is in mourning.

You may really be in the dark about what is happening in his life and yet you judge him. This is an example of the kind of darkness that comes from ignorance (as I, unfortunately, know all too well).

If you are led to places of darkness within your own thoughts, feelings, or judgements, pray that God's light leads you to seek the truth and guide you to act in loving ways based on that truth.

Take a break. Return to your place of quiet retreat and expand your reflection to include the darkness in the world around you. Spend time prayerfully considering a darkness in your community that you worry or even think about regularly. This could be one person, like the untreated mentally ill man who routinely cries out against unseen enemies across the street from my apartment, or it could be a large group, like the growing number of people who are living in tents or cars because their circumstances have rendered them homeless. Maybe you are drawn to a concern for abused or neglected children or those trapped in the prison of addiction. These are people who, like many others, are living in darkness.

Prayerfully read these words from the Prophet Isaiah and ask the Spirit to bring to mind times when God has rescued you from the darkness of sadness, grief, ignorance, or misunderstanding. Read the passage a second time, asking for God's light to lead you to a more enlightened understanding of another's darkness so that you may receive the gift of empathy.

> I [the Lord] will lead the blind by a road they do not know, by paths they have not known I will guide them. I will turn the darkness before them into light, the rough places into level ground. These are the things I will do, and I will not forsake them. (Isa 42:16)

Conclude your time of prayerful reflection by reading the following passage and then praying for the ability to fulfill these words.

> No one after lighting a lamp puts it under the bushel basket, but on the lampstand, and it gives light to all in the house. In the same way, let your light shine before others, so that they may see your good works and give glory to your Father in heaven. (Matt 5:15–16)

WHERE THERE IS DARKNESS, LIGHT

Darkness cannot drive out darkness: only light can do that.
—Martin Luther King Jr.[1]

A Time for Action

During your time of reflection, you probably identified some areas of darkness within your community. Choose one area that gives you concern, a darkness that has remained in your heart and mind, a darkness you feel called to help dispel. Once you have done this, gather a group of friends to help you discover how the Spirit can guide you to bring light to the places in your community that might be in darkness. You may be surprised at how difficult this job is. Remember your own darknesses, blind spots, and implicit assumptions. Take an inventory of the resources that you might have access to (such as an easily accessible internet connection) that those experiencing this kind of darkness do not have.

Doing a fair bit of research is a useful way to reinforce your call for action. For example, getting help from government programs is often a complex (and sometimes convoluted) process. There will most likely be forms, protocols, and bureaucracy to deal with. You need the time and the ability to find the right departments, talk to the right administrators, and fill out the right paperwork. A person without a home or with limited finances most likely won't have the resources to take all these necessary steps. It can even be so difficult that you might not be able to take all the necessary steps on your own. Where should you go for help? Look at the places where the Spirit may already be at work through the ministries of both church and secular nonprofits. What kind of help do these organizations offer? Are they located near the areas of darkness to which they seek to bring light? How do they make their work known to those who need help? These are just a few of the questions you will need to answer if you want to shine light on the darkness you have decided to confront.

---

1. King, *Gift of Love*, 49.

Though it might be a tedious and frustrating process, remember this information gathering is a holy process. It should be conducted prayerfully, for through it you are asking God to lead you out of the darkness of ignorance about others' suffering and into the light of compassion. We must always remember that offering light in the darkness is not just a way to help people in need. It is primarily a way to "walk in love as Christ loved us" (Eph 5:2) and to let our light shine before others so that we might bring glory to God (Matt 5:16).

After this time of information gathering, take the actions you need to take using the help and resources you have found available to you. When you meet with your group, ask everyone to commit to ongoing prayer for those whose experience with darkness you've been called to explore. Pray for the courage and the discipline to step out in faith to bring at least a bit of light into the darkness.

> If you offer your food to the hungry and satisfy the needs
> of the afflicted, then your light shall rise in the darkness
> and your gloom be like the noonday. (Isa 58:10)

OPTIONAL ACTIVITY

Watch the seventeen-minute movie *Chuj Boys of Summer*.[2]

This short film follows a teen migrant named Yakin as he adjusts to his new life in Telluride, Colorado. He is from Guatemala and only speaks Chuj (pronounced "chew"), the language of his Indigenous people. This is a coming-of-age story featuring non-professional actors, most of whom are Guatemalan immigrants. It is reflective of the real-life experiences of one of the movie's creators and others in this small mountain community.[3]

---

2. *Chuj Boys of Summer* is available to view online (link in the bibliography under Walker-Silverman).

3. Garcia-Navarro, "Student Film."

7

Where There Is Sadness, Joy

The fruit of the Spirit is love, joy, peace, patience, kindness, generosity, faithfulness, gentleness, and self-control. There is no law against such things.

—Galatians 5:22

FOUNDATION

Joy is one of the fruits of living in the Spirit. It is a gift. But it is also a gift that is most often received when we discipline ourselves to seek it. Joy is not mere happiness, which is dependent upon the events that surround us, but rather, a state of being. Having the gift of joy, being a joy-filled and joyful person, does not mean that we never encounter tragedy or experience times of sadness. It also does not mean that we are unmoved by the suffering of others or that we wear a perpetual grin on our faces no matter what is happening around us. In some ways, in fact, having the gift of joy means that we are more in touch with our own sufferings and the sufferings of others. According to the late author Rachel Held Evens, joy does not keep us from feeling other emotions or being moved by painful situations. Instead, joy sharpens our ability to feel everything more fully. The opposite of joy is not sadness or anger; it is cynicism.[1]

> Cynicism is a powerful anesthetic we use to numb ourselves to pain, but which also, by its nature, numbs us to truth and joy. Grief is healthy. Even anger can be healthy. But numbing ourselves with cynicism in an effort to avoid feeling those things is not.[2]

Perhaps it is not even too far a stretch to say that living with joy helps us to be wholly human in the holy way God created us to be.

But how can we as individuals, and as the church community, share joy with those to whom we are reaching out—especially those who are experiencing times of great pain, doubt, and darkness? We cannot sow seeds of joy unless we are joyful people ourselves. The apostles and believers who made up the earliest congregations were filled with joy even during times of persecution. This joy is what drew others to them. Joy, it seems, was at the very heart of the earliest communities of faith.

> At its very heart was the experience of joy and gladness, as evidenced by the repeated use of these words and their derivatives. Joy is hardly a piece of nontheological or amoral trivia in the story of the early church; it not only fuels the witness of the disciples in the world but serves as one of the central and manifest expressions of their life together and of the presence of the Holy Spirit. Joy is the church's response not only to daily healings and conversions but also to being accorded worthy to suffer shame for Christ's name. According to Luke, the church's response to rejection and persecution was that "the disciples were filled with joy and with the Holy Spirit." (Acts 13:52)[3]

The earliest Christians apparently were able to sow seeds of joy by living lives of joy themselves in spite of (and sometimes even because of) the hardships they encountered.

1. Evans, *Searching for Sunday*, 222.
2. Evans, *Searching for Sunday*, 222.
3. Stone, *Evangelism After Christendom*, 103.

I recently read a sermon preached by the Rev. Dr. Sam Wells of Duke University, a homily about Easter joy. He spoke about what it means to live by the discipline of joy. Some of the qualities he mentioned were: hope, community, and living beyond fear.[4]

These words seemed to concisely describe the life of the early church. The early Christians were filled with hope, lovingly committed to their community, living with generosity, and existing in peace despite their fears.

> Our message of the gospel came to you not in word only, but also in power and in the Holy Spirit and with full conviction; just as you know what kind of persons we proved to be among you for your sake. And you became imitators of us and of the Lord, for in spite of persecution you received the word with joy inspired by the Holy Spirit, so that you became an example to all the believers in Macedonia and in Achaia. (1 Thess 1:5–7)

The early church shared joy all with those around them.

> All who believed were together and had all things in common; they would sell their possessions and goods and distribute the proceeds to all, as any had need. Day by day, as they spent much time together in the temple, they broke bread at home and ate their food with glad and generous hearts, praising God and having the goodwill of all the people. And day by day the Lord added to their number those who were being saved. (Acts 2:44–47)

Perhaps one reason for the people of the early church's ability to live in joy was their general orientation toward the other rather than the self. In Paul's second letter to the believers in Corinth, he says:

> We want you to know, brothers and sisters, about the grace of God that has been granted to the churches of Macedonia; for during a severe ordeal of affliction, their abundant joy and their extreme poverty have overflowed in a wealth of generosity on their part. For, as I can testify, they voluntarily gave according to their means, and

---

4. Wells, "Discipline of Joy."

> even beyond their means, begging us earnestly for the privilege of sharing in this ministry to the saints. (2 Cor 8:1–3)

This all means that if we are to pray to bring joy to places of sadness, we must first become people of joy ourselves, and we are called to do this within the context of community

A Time for Reflection

Lord, make us instruments of your peace. Where there is sadness, let us sow joy.

Once again, commit to keeping this petition in your heart and mind and repeating it often.

> When a woman is in labor, she has pain, because her hour has come. But when her child is born, she no longer remembers the anguish because of the joy of having brought a human being into the world. (John 16:21)

Take the opportunity this week to reflect upon times during the past when you have experienced joy. If you are a mother maybe you can relate with the illustration Jesus shared with his disciples. Even if you have never given birth, you can probably remember a time in your life when a difficult or painful experience brought forth new life or preceded a time of joy.

Consider the following questions and note your responses. Did an event or a relationship ever lead you beyond a sense of happiness and into real joy?

_____
_____
_____
_____

WHERE THERE IS SADNESS, JOY

Have you ever experienced joy—a sense of God's presence that reassured you that you are loved and that God has not abandoned you—even during a time of suffering or sadness?

_____

_____

_____

_____

Spend some time prayerfully remembering the events that just came to mind. Ask the Spirit to guide you into a deeper understanding of what you experienced and how it resulted in a sense of joy or how joy was present in the midst of it.

Now, slowly and prayerfully read the following passage from Scripture.

> As the Father has loved me, so I have loved you; abide in my love. If you keep my commandments, you will abide in my love, just as I have kept my Father's commandments and abide in his love. I have said these things to you so that my joy may be in you, and that your joy may be complete. (John 15: 9–11)

After your first reading, ask yourself what word or phrase captured your attention as you read. Now read it a second time, and imagine what your life would be like if you made a conscious effort to *abide in Christ's love*. Let your ideas about this kind of abiding guide your behaviors over the next few days. Whatever disappointment or resentment comes your way—for example, when you get frustrated because you've failed to complete a task or haven't received recognition when you thought it was your due—say to yourself, "I am still God's beloved."

Joy comes from knowing that we are loved, then being able to share that love with one another, no matter the circumstances of our lives. Prayerfully consider the ways you experience the love of Christ in your daily life. Are you made most aware of this love during times of prayer? Does the love and care of others reassure you of the Lord's love?

How do/can you spend more of your time abiding in this love that leads to joy? Note at least a few ideas for doing this in the space below.

_____

_____

_____

_____

End your time of reflection with a prayer of thanksgiving for the gift of joy.

A Time for Action

> *A joyful heart is the normal result of a heart burning with love. She gives most who gives with joy.*
>
> —MOTHER TERESA[5]

Take time today to make two lists. Title one "What I have received from the generosity of others," and title the other "What I can give away today."

We have all benefited a tremendous amount from the generosity of others. You might need to limit your first list to the recent past. As you write this list, think of what was required of your donors. How did they give you a particular gift? Did they seem happy to do so?

A MEMORY

> *One of the generous people in my young life was a truck driver who worked at the same resort where my father was employed. I remember he often sat on his front porch as we came home from school. He would stop whatever he was doing to listen to our tales and complaints. He never seemed burdened by our presence despite the fact that*

---

5. Mother Teresa of Calcutta, *In the Heart*, 27.

none of us led the kind of interesting lives that would have commanded his attention. Even though it seemed like a small thing at the time, it was a large enough generosity that I remember it all these years later.

Challenge yourself to fill your first list with gifts of generosity both large and small. Before you begin your second list, take some time to center yourself and pray for guidance. Note what you can generously give away today. Try to think beyond cleaning out your closet for charity and consider other kinds of giveaways. Maybe you can give up some of your time to call a shut-in or bake cookies for someone who writes materials such as the one you are reading now. Whatever it is, be generous and live without fear of loss or the need for thanks or appreciation.

After making your two lists and acting on the second one, take some time to reflect on your experience. Make some notes on what you may have learned, and give thanks for it all to God in prayer.

_____
_____
_____
_____

Consider how this exercise has freed or prepared you to sow seeds of joy. By acknowledging how much we have received (not just from God, but also from one another) and then giving without fear of the cost, we have been introduced to the kind of joy we are called to live into as individuals and as the church. This is the life we are invited to embrace and share, joining with others to "find ourselves" by stretching out the arms of our minds and hearts.[6] And in doing so we will "find ourselves, Christ shaped, cross shaped, at the intersection of the past, present, and future of God's time and our own time."[7]

---

6. Wright, *Case for the Psalms*, 141.
7. Wright, *Case for the Psalms*, 141.

If you found this exercise in joy and giving helpful, share it with a few faithful friends. Then, ask them to join you in some activity of generosity that can be done with joy and with the intention of bringing joy to others. This does not need to be something that will change the sociopolitical landscape—like negotiating a lasting peace in the Middle East (although that would produce great joy). It can be as simple as a pop-up ice-cream social at a homeless encampment or a hymn sing at a nursing home. Just see where the Spirit will lead you to sow seeds of joy where others may be experiencing sadness.

Joy is the infallible sign of the presence of God.
—Pierre Teilhard de Chardin[8]

---

8. InspiringQuotes, "Pierre Teilhard de Chardin."

8

Grant That We May Not So Much Seek to Be Consoled as to Console; to Be Understood as to Understand; to Be Loved as to Love

FOUNDATION

I highly recommend that you read the short YA novel *Coaltown Jesus* by Ron Koertge as you continue to pray and live out of this prayer. The plot centers on Walker, a grieving teen, who suddenly experiences visits from Jesus. Jesus cannot be seen by anyone else. He does not work any miracles or have any startling words of wisdom for Walker, whose life has been upended by the death of his older brother. Jesus is just present. And through his presence Walker finds healing and hope. I have given this book to teens who are experiencing loss. I reread it myself on occasion. It provides a powerful image of what it means to be present in the life of another. I have been moved to action by it in very meaningful ways.

To console, to understand, and to love requires that we be present for those who are grieving, those who have not been listened to, and those who feel unloved or unlovable. Jesus gave up the glories of heaven to take on human flesh. He walked with us amongst all of the chaos and confusion, pleasure and pain. And he calls on us to walk like him.

> Let the same mind be in you that was in Christ Jesus, who, though he was in the form of God, did not regard equality with God as something to be exploited, but emptied himself, taking the form of a slave, being born in human likeness. (Phil 2:5–7)

Obviously, these are big sandals to fill. Nevertheless, the Holy Spirit has empowered every one of us to step alongside Christ and reflect his light onto the lives of those around us. Like light being fractured and colored by a prism, we too become slivers of the all-encompassing light that is Christ, each uniquely refracting that light in the very specific ways for which we were created. And so, as we pray to be able to offer consolation, understanding and love, we also pray for the opportunities to do so in our own limited but wholly original ways. We pray for this not because we think we have the wisdom or the ability to save the world. No, that is the job of the Savior, and Jesus has that well in hand, thank you very much. Instead, we are called to enter into the roiling waters of life with those who have felt loss, those who have been ignored, those who have been unloved, and to hold them close. We are not called to distance ourselves from those in need by setting ourselves up as "experts" with all the answers. Instead, we are called to be followers of the one who saves us, to be imitators of his way of being in the world. We are called to an incarnational love that is modeled on the love Christ has given us. And we are called, in all of this, as members of the body of Christ—as interconnected and mutually dependent brothers and sisters in God's family.

> Therefore, be imitators of God, as beloved children, and live in love, as Christ loved us. (Eph 5:1–2)

A Time for Reflection

Grant that we may not so much seek to be consoled as to console; to be understood as to understand; to be loved as to love.

As you work your way through the rest of this chapter be sure to remember and frequently repeat this portion of the prayer.

Take some time with the parable of the Good Samaritan:

> "A man was going down from Jerusalem to Jericho, and fell into the hands of robbers, who stripped him, beat him, and went away, leaving him half dead. Now by chance a priest was going down that road; and when he saw him, he passed by on the other side. So likewise a Levite, when he came to the place and saw him, passed by on the other side. But a Samaritan while traveling came near him; and when he saw him, he was moved with pity. He went to him and bandaged his wounds, having poured oil and wine on them. Then he put him on his own animal, brought him to an inn, and took care of him. The next day he took out two denarii, gave them to the innkeeper, and said, 'Take care of him; and when I come back, I will repay you whatever more you spend.'" (Luke 10:25–37)

Slowly and prayerfully read this story while imagining the locations and each of the people described in it. What does the terrain look like? Is the road rocky? What's the weather like? Now imagine each character with as much specificity as possible. Go beyond what they look like and try to imagine them as full human beings with particular beliefs, gifts, problems, etc. Let these images rest with you and then return to this text on another day. You may want to make some notes about the images you've imagined in the space below.

The location

___

The traveler

___

Lord, Make Us Instruments of Your Peace

The robbers

_____

The priest

_____

The Levite

_____

The Samaritan

_____

The innkeeper

_____

Now read the parable again, this time focusing on the relationship between the injured man, the Samaritan, and the innkeeper. What do you notice? Make note of the way that the Samaritan finds the injured man, helps him, and then allows another to continue that care.

_____
_____
_____
_____

How does this speak to you about the movement of the Spirit and the necessity for community?

_____
_____
_____
_____

Allow all that you have imagined and considered to linger with you for a few days before moving on to the next activity.

After spending time picturing and wondering about this parable, return to it one last time. As you read it, try to imagine it in a contemporary setting. Where does it happen? Who are the attackers? Who are those who pass by the injured man? Who is the one who helps him? And to what kind of safe place is he taken? How do modern lifestyles and technologies figure in to the way this story now unfolds? Give yourself the time to really imagine this story in such a way that it becomes a believable scenario—a story that could happen in your own community.

If you feel led, write your new parable in the space below.

_____
_____
_____
_____
_____
_____
_____
_____

A Time for Action

As you continue to explore this section of the prayer, I invite you to take a risk and reach out to someone who is alone, grieving, or feeling misunderstood or unloved. Begin by prayerfully considering the members of your own congregation. I am sure that as you do this, more than a few names will pop into your head. Don't focus on people you think you can help because of any of your particular gifts, resources, or advantages. Allow the Spirit to tug on your heart for someone who just needs to be heard. I am embarrassed to say that whenever I have tried this sort of thing, the Spirit immediately brings to mind people I would rather not spend time with. I am much more drawn to the elderly widow who is so appreciative of any offering or the lonely teen who likes to do the kind of things I do. But this is not about finding someone who will make us feel good about ourselves, this is about finding someone who needs a particular kind of love and who possibly can't or won't be able to give us anything in return. Maybe it's someone who seems emotionally needy and continues to commemorate the deaths of family members, with many tears, for decades. Maybe it is someone whose grief reawakens your own griefs and losses, or maybe it is someone with a chronic illness for which there is no cure. Whoever the Spirit brings to mind, consider reaching out to them.

If you are willing to take this risk, begin with prayer. Pray for the person whom you feel led to contact. Pray for the Spirit's guidance in how to approach them. Take as much time as you need. Depending on your circumstances and the context of your community, how you proceed will be up to you as you feel led. What follows is an example of one simple form of reaching out.

> *After your church's worship service one week, approach the person with whom you wish to connect and say, "Hello, how are you?" Then take the time to listen to their answer. If they speak of any specific needs or complaints, ask if you can include them in your daily prayers (and then do so). Check in with them the following week, saying something like, "You've been on my mind and in my prayers this week, how are you doing today?" Continue to be present to them during this after-service time each week. At some point, depending on their circumstances, you can invite them to join you in some other aspect of church life you think they might enjoy. For example, if you attend a weekly Bible study, invite them to join with you and make a point of introducing them to the other members of the group. Or maybe you find out you have a shared interest you can enjoy together sometime. Remembering how my husband and I had once talked about what fun we had as kids playing miniature golf, some church friends invited me to join their family for such an outing a couple of months after my husband died. Listening (on their part) led to fellowship*

around a fun activity for us all, and no small amount of healing for me. The point is, no matter where your gift of presence leads (mini golf, axe throwing, or even just offering friendship to someone who routinely stands alone at coffee hour), you have begun to explore what it means to live out your call as a member of the body of Christ.

Keep an informal journal about your experience offering consolation, understanding, and love. Note how you were led to the person you reached out to. Describe your feelings of resistance or encouragement as you took on this challenge. And reflect on what you received from this new relationship in spite of working not to ask for anything in return for your efforts.

It is a great consolation for me to remember that the Lord, to whom I had drawn near in humble and child-like faith, has suffered and died for me, and that He will look on me in love and compassion.

—Wolfgang Amadeus Mozart[1]

---

1. SpiritualRay, "Profound Christian Quotes."

9

For It Is in Giving That We Receive; It Is in Pardoning That We Are Pardoned; and It Is in Dying That We Are Born to Eternal Life

FOUNDATION

The last words of this prayer are perhaps the most difficult to think about. I am reminded of the old joke in which a Sunday school teacher asks her class, "By a show of hands, how many of you want to go to heaven?" All but one child raises their hands. She then asks the one child without a raised hand, "Why don't you want to go to heaven?" He responds, "Oh, I do. I just thought you meant *right now.*"

The good news, news that this prayer reminds us of, is that eternal life does begin right now. And while we may receive a clearer picture of just what that means after our physical death, we are still invited to live into God's eternal love each and every day. One way of doing this, the Prayer of St. Francis seems to be saying, is to die each day to the ways of the world so that we can more fully live in God's kingdom of shalom—even before it has achieved completion.

We die to the ways of the world each time we give rather than seeking to get. We can give not only by bestowing things, but by sharing our time or our talents in ways that bring light and hope, unity and joy, to others. We can also give by offering pardon rather than the collecting grudges or resentments. Each time we die to selfish impulses, reactions based on fear or distrust or the need for control, we step a little more into that eternal peace and joy of life with God.

Dying to that which separates me from the love of God needs to be a daily activity. It is the reason why I love the Prayer of St. Francis so much. It gives me a path to follow, a way of dying that does not bring destruction, but instead clears away that which keeps me separated from abundant life—a life that is abundant not because of material goods but because it is filled with love and joy, because it blesses me with meaningful relationships and opportunities to use who I am and what I can do with real purpose, without restraint or insecurity.

Dying so that we might have eternal life is less about giving up and more about letting go of that which separates us from God's love and from meaningful relationships with one another. When we can let go of those things, even some of the time, we can experience God's gift of eternal life right here and right now. We can live in God's kingdom of shalom.

A Time for Reflection

For it is in giving that we receive; it is in pardoning that we are pardoned; and it is in dying that we are born to eternal life.

Repeat this reminder and promise from the prayer as often as possible throughout the days ahead.

Settle yourself in a quiet place where you can be undisturbed for the next twenty or thirty minutes.

Prayerfully read these words from Jesus.

> Jesus answered them, "The hour has come for the Son of Man to be glorified. Very truly, I tell you, unless a grain

of wheat falls into the earth and dies, it remains just a single grain; but if it dies, it bears much fruit. Those who love their life lose it, and those who hate their life in this world will keep it for eternal life. (John 12:23–25)

As you read it the first time, try to do so in a completely literal way. Imagine a grain of wheat going into the earth. Picture the way that the grain decomposes so that it can be remade into a sprout that pokes its head above the surface of the earth. Follow its maturation as roots form in the earth and the sprout turns into a stalk that brings forth a head covered in multiple grains. Spend some time wondering about how the single grain develops into a plant that bears "much fruit." Does this seem miraculous to you? No matter what the scientific explanations are, does this whole process still have an air of mystery about it?

Now, read the passage again and listen for the ways Jesus is giving his disciples hints about his coming death and resurrection. After this second reading, take some time to wonder about how the death and resurrection has borne more fruit than if Jesus had remained alive until a natural death. What did this fruit look like immediately after Jesus died? What did this fruit look like in the first decade or so after his death and resurrection?

Read this passage one last time. When you are finished, spend as much time as you need considering what fruit the death and resurrection of Jesus has produced in your own life. Try to go beyond the obvious—eternal life, for example—and think about the specific ways your life has been fruitful because of this world-changing gift. Are there fruits you have ignored or not tended? What changes do you feel led to make because of this time of prayer with these words?

End your time of reflection by praying the Prayer of St. Francis in light of what you have just discovered.

A Time for Action

The end of our physical lives is only one way that we humans experience death. We face other kinds of endings and loss during our lifetimes. The end of a marriage forces us to face the death of a relationship that we thought would help define our lives. Retirement can feel like the death of our purpose. Serious illness or the loss of physical or mental abilities can kill certain dreams we may have had for our future. These are just a few of the deaths we can experience during our earthly lifetimes. They are deaths that we must mourn before we can find a way to live with joy.

Perhaps you have already lived through one of these kinds of death or are moving through one of them now. At times like these, it is difficult to remember the gift of eternal life or to see the opportunities for healing and wholeness. But part of the fruit of Christ's death and resurrection, fruit that can nourish and comfort you during times of loss, can be found in his body, the church. If you are experiencing any kind of death in your life, I urge you to reach out to members of your faith community and allow them to walk with you during this painful time.

We have little control over the kinds of death just described. But, through prayer and the love of fellow believers, we can find new life after such experiences. As we consider this last portion of the Prayer of Saint Francis however, I would like us to consider and act on the aspects of our lives we do have some measure of control over, especially those parts of our existence that really need to be put to death.

Take some time to prayerfully consider any habits, attitudes or behaviors that keep you from more fully living in God's kingdom of shalom. Reflect on what may be keeping you from enjoying the blessings of eternal life right here and right now. Fearlessly ask yourself what still prevents you from being an instrument of God's peace. These can be anything from a feud with a family member to an attachment to a long-held hurt; a habit of over-consuming that prevents you from sharing what you have with others or a long-held belief that everyone around you is smarter, thinner, holier, etc. than you. Whatever it is that is holding you back from more fully engaging in a relationship with your loving Savior and with the people around you, make note of it in the space below.

LORD, MAKE US INSTRUMENTS OF YOUR PEACE

_____
_____
_____
_____
_____
_____

After you have made your list, think about what your life would look like (what would change) if you could kill off any or all of the beliefs and behaviors you've identified. Make note of the images and ideas that come to mind in the space below.

_____
_____
_____
_____

This is the tough part. Make a plan for eliminating at least one of the beliefs or behaviors you've identified. Write it down. Commit to following your plan. It may take some time. When I think of what keeps us from more fully accepting God's love and living out of that love, I think of Bermuda grass: it is really, really hard to kill. Here is a bit of Bermuda I am struggling to kill in my own life: I hold on to memories of bad experiences and personal hurts. When I am asked to help with a project, lead a class, or participate in some way with a person or group with whom I've had a past hurtful experience—even one from years ago—I immediately relive the experience that wounded me. It rekindles the hurt I felt at the time and prevents me from moving on. I know I need to put this petty, self-pitying habit to death. Recently, when these kinds of thoughts pop up, I silence them by asking God to forgive my unforgiveness and open my mind to the new life-giving opportunities that are being offered to me. It works—most of the time. Okay, some of the time. But I have committed to keeping at it. If

FOR IT IS IN GIVING THAT WE RECEIVE

I can do it, so can you. Just keep going, and remember you don't have to do it alone. Tell a faithful friend about what you are doing and ask them to pray for you and hold you accountable.

_____

_____

_____

_____

_____

Return to your commitment in a few weeks to check in on your progress. How has this death (or your struggle with it) opened your heart to God and helped you to be more of an instrument of God's peace each day? Don't beat yourself up if you are progressing more slowly than you had hoped. Rejoice and be glad. And remember, "greater is he that is in you, than he that is in the world" (1 John 4:4).

> *The familiar and the habitual are so falsely reassuring, and most of us make our homes there permanently. The new is always by definition unfamiliar and untested, so God, life, destiny, suffering have to give us a push—usually a big one—or we will not go.*
>
> —Richard Rohr[1]

---

1. Rohr, *Falling Upward*, xvii.

10

Amen: Some Closing Thoughts

Did you notice that you received something from participating in the previous tasks? If so, what did you gain while you sought to sow seeds of peace, love, pardon, faith, hope, light, and joy? Did you receive a greater sense of your specific call to live as a follower of Jesus? Did you gain knowledge about the world around you and the needs of those living in it? Do you feel more empathetic, hopeful, or at peace? Take a few minutes to think back over your experience with this prayer and wonder about the ways you may have grown or changed.

HOW WILL YOU CONTINUE TO PRAY AND LIVE AS AN INSTRUMENT OF GOD'S PEACE?

What, if anything, did you discover during your time of wondering? I hope that you saw that God is calling you to be an instrument of peace in ways both big and small and that you have been given everything you need to do this. I also hope that this time with the prayer has made you realize that even though you are "fearfully and wonderfully made" (Ps 139:14), you are not called to do any of this on your own. You are called to be one instrument of God's peace within an orchestra of instruments, all with different tones and timbres but coming together to play the beautiful music of God's love. This, I think, is the holy gift that comes when we abandon radical individualism and accept that in God's kingdom of shalom, we are all in continual relationship with one another as givers and receivers, lovers and the beloved. So, as we strive to pray and live out the call of this prayer, let us be mindful that we are not really praying it by ourselves. We are praying with the communion of saints in its entirety, here on earth and in heaven.

The time you have just spent focusing on the Prayer of St. Francis has, among other things, probably made you more sensitive to the pains and problems of the world. How has that made you feel? Sometimes, when we experience pain and see the suffering that so many around us endure, it may be tempting to wish for a comic book superhero to solve our problems or rescue those in danger. But even if such beings existed, the kind of help they would offer would be nothing more than a quick fix, a fix often grounded in revenge, and a fix that would need to be repeated time and time again. There's a reason Gotham has to have a Bat-Signal: what Batman offers has no lasting effects. Evildoers keep reappearing and he must be summoned time and time again. The superhero becomes more like the player of Whack-A-Mole than the provider of healing and hope.

It is good to remember at this point that as much as we pray to be active followers of Jesus by giving and pardoning like he did, we are still just human beings. We are not superheroes. We are sinners—redeemed sinners, but sinners all the same. . . . "For all have sinned and fall short of the glory of God" (Rom 3:23).

The good news is Jesus has not called us to be his followers all on our own. We have been given the Holy Spirit to dwell within us, to encourage and empower us, and we have been given one another. We are never alone. We need God—Father, Son, and Holy Spirit—and we need our brothers and sisters in Christ. Thankfully, we have God and one another to walk with us on this journey we call life.

As we end this time of reflection and action based on the Prayer of St. Francis, we should be reminded of our own needs as well as our gifts, and of our interconnectedness with other believers. As we pray to become instruments of his peace, in all of the ways described in this prayer, we do so with the encouragement and empowerment of the Holy Spirit along with the support of our community of faith.

> *No one is so rich that he does not need another's help; no one so poor as not to be useful in some way to his fellow man; and the disposition to ask assistance from others with confidence and to grant it with kindness is part of our very nature.*
>
> —Pope Leo XIII[1]

A FINAL REFLECTION

Contrast the image of the superhero with who Jesus calls his followers to be. Slowly and prayerfully read Luke 10:1–11, 16–20.

> After this the Lord appointed seventy others and sent them on ahead of him in pairs to every town and place where he himself intended to go. He said to them, "The harvest is plentiful, but the laborers are few; therefore ask the Lord of the harvest to send out laborers into his harvest. Go on your way. See, I am sending you out like lambs into the midst of wolves. Carry no purse, no bag, no sandals; and greet no one on the road. Whatever house you enter, first say, 'Peace to this house!' And if anyone is there who shares in peace, your peace will rest on that person; but if not, it will return to you. Remain in the same house, eating and drinking whatever they provide, for the laborer deserves to be paid. Do not move about from house to house. Whenever you enter a town and its people welcome you, eat what is set before you; cure the sick who are there, and say to them, 'The kingdom of God has come near to you.' But whenever you enter a town and they do not welcome you, go out into its streets and say, 'Even the dust of your town that clings to our

---

1. Leo XIII, *Graves de communi re*, 16.

feet, we wipe off in protest against you. Yet know this: the kingdom of God has come near.' . . .

"Whoever listens to you listens to me, and whoever rejects you rejects me, and whoever rejects me rejects the one who sent me." The seventy returned with joy, saying, "Lord, in your name even the demons submit to us!" He said to them, "I watched Satan fall from heaven like a flash of lightning. See, I have given you authority to tread on snakes and scorpions, and over all the power of the enemy; and nothing will hurt you. Nevertheless, do not rejoice at this, that the spirits submit to you, but rejoice that your names are written in heaven." (Luke 10:1–11, 16–20)

Now, read it a second time with a pencil in hand. Underline verses that describe how Jesus sends the disciples out into the world. Circle what Jesus tells them to do when they arrive at their destinations. What stands out to you when you look over your markings? Does anything in this passage make you uncomfortable? Do you wonder if this kind of reaching out is possible in today's world? How do the outreach and evangelism programs at your church mirror or stand in contrast to the way Jesus sent his followers into the world? In light of this reading, do you think that you and your community are be being called into a new or different way of sharing the good news and offering help and healing to the world around you? Use the space below to make note of what you came up with during this exercise and, if you feel led to do so, share thoughts with your pastor and others in your congregation.

_____
_____
_____
_____

LORD, MAKE US INSTRUMENTS OF YOUR PEACE

A FINAL ACTIVITY (OR TWO)

There is a reason that people in times of pain or stress are drawn to community. We were created to live in community and, through the power of the Holy Spirit, to love, nurture, and abide with one another in both good and bad times.[2] Our risen Lord has called us to grow as a part of his body the way branches grow from the vine from which they sprout (John 15:5). Our Lord sent the Holy Spirit to all of us for comfort and empowerment. We have been invited to share those gifts with one another as if we are living in the fulfillment of God's kingdom as it now is in heaven (Luke 11:2–4). We can only live this way if we commit ourselves each day to striving to not just pray for the "life to come" (1 Tim 4: 8–10) but to embody it in the here and now. We are called, with the help of the Holy Spirit and our brothers and sisters in Christ, to a sacred life that is at once both prayerful and active.

Peace, love, and justice are not merely hopeful fancies for a future time, in other words, but are manifest in the present moment: "The kingdom of God is . . . righteousness [or justice] and peace and joy in the Holy Spirit (Rom. 14:17)."[3]

Living in true Christian community is not always (or often?) going to be easy. Every individual making up the Christian community is a unique creation of God who has also inherited or accumulated a good deal of baggage from their family, their culture, and their particular life experiences. You can view this as a problem or proclaim it as a blessing that calls all of us—complete with our gifts and our brokenness—into the blend of unity and diversity we call the body of Christ. I invite you to now dive into the body of Christ by hosting a discussion group or throwing a party and inviting some members of your congregation whom you don't know that well. Perhaps the people you invite come from different backgrounds or live in a different part of the city or town you are living in. Whatever the case, invite people you might not normally

---

2. Gorman, *Becoming the Gospel*, 19.
3. Gorman, *Becoming the Gospel*, 33.

think of inviting. Here are some suggestions for a couple of ways of doing this.

Option 1. A Gathering for Discussion of the Prayer of St. Francis with Others

Set a time and date to invite a group of people (no more than twelve) to join you for a discussion of this prayer. Try to make your guest list as varied as possible. Extend you invitation to people from a variety of age groups, cultural or ethnic backgrounds, and political persuasions.

After a short time for casual conversation and introductions, give each person a copy of the Prayer Attributed to St. Francis. Ask one person to read it aloud. After a short period of silence ask this question: "What word or phrase captured your attention or confused, excited, or troubled you?" After everyone has a chance to share (without interruption or comment by others) ask someone else to read the prayer again. Following a time of silence, ask: "Do you hear a call to action from any of these petitions? If so, what?" After everyone has a chance to share (without interruption or comment by others) allow for a time of open discussion.

Share one of the "Time for Reflection" activities with the entire group. Make sure you've made copies of the reflection you've chosen and have paper and pencils available. When everyone has completed this exercise, encourage them to share their insights and responses.

If people seem to have enjoyed this experience, and you feel called to do so, use this as a jumping off point to work through this book together. You could suggest everyone read one chapter at a time and then gather every other week or so to participate in the action suggested in that chapter or in an activity that you devise to help all of you better connect with that portion of the prayer.

End your time together with prayer.

Option 2. Throw a Party

If your home or yard is large enough to accommodate about a dozen people, great. If not, arrange to meet at a park or some other communal space. Try to make your guest list as varied as possible. Extend your invitation to people from a variety of age groups, cultural or ethnic backgrounds, and political persuasions.

When you extend your invitation, ask each person to bring a food item to share that is special to them in some way. It could be a dish that is representative of their ethnic background or a favorite from their childhood. It could also be their favorite comfort food or something they associate with a special event or time in their life. Encourage people to be creative and let them know that they will be asked to share the story of their food choice with the rest of the partygoers. You'll need to supply the plates, napkins, drinks, etc.

Once everyone has gathered and you've had some time to say hello, introduce folks who don't know each other. Ask someone to offer a prayer of thanks and then let the sampling of the food begin. As host, you will need to guide the mealtime conversation so that everyone gets the chance to talk about the food they brought and why it is significant to them. Each person should be allowed to speak without interruption or commentary by others. When everyone has had a chance to talk, encourage a more general conversation with questions about what has been shared.

Ask someone to read the Prayer of St. Francis to the group. After a brief silence, say something like, "Through the sharing of food we have experienced a bit of what we all share in common and a bit of our differing tastes, cultural backgrounds, and ways of celebrating. The same can be said about how we hear and respond to the movement of the Holy Spirit within our lives. With that in mind, what part of this prayer are you most drawn to, that you want to explore more or commit more of your prayer and service time to?" Allow time for discussion. Then ask something like, "What part of this prayer gives you the most pause? Which petition causes you to feel the most resistance?" Allow time for discussion.

AMEN: SOME CLOSING THOUGHTS

After everyone has had a chance to take part in the discussion, ask something like, "If we got together again, what would you like to see us do together? Would you like to spend more time with this prayer by sharing a (this) book together? Or would you like to meet together to take part in a specific outreach or mission project, Bible study, or fellowship event?" If the group seems to want to gather again but isn't sure how to proceed you can suggest that you contact them via email during the next week with a couple of ideas. If they do come up with a plan be sure to follow up with specific details as soon as possible.

AND, FINALLY . . .

Thank you for exploring the Prayer of St. Francis with me. I hope that the words of this prayer as well as the exercises and experiences suggested in this book have been a blessing for you. My prayer is that we may all continue to grow in our desire to become instruments of God's peace and to act on that desire in the way that we speak and the way that we live each and every day.

> May the God of steadfastness and encouragement grant you to live in harmony with one another, in accordance with Christ Jesus, so that together you may with one voice glorify the God and Father of our Lord Jesus Christ. (Rom 15:5–6)

Bibliography

101 Studios. "Burden Trailer (2020) Forest Whitaker, Garret Hedlund Movie." YouTube, Oct. 24, 2019. https://www.youtube.com/watch?v=gTDXiVbwqxw.

AZ Quotes. "Lewis B. Smedes Quotes." https://www.azquotes.com/author/13725-Lewis_B_Smedes.

The Book of Common Prayer of the Episcopal Church. New York: Church Publishing, 1979.

Christianity.com Editorial Staff. "What Is the Prayer of St. Francis? Origin and Meaning." Christianity.com. Updated Dec. 21, 2020. https://www.christianity.com/wiki/prayer/what-is-the-prayer-of-st-francis-origin-and-meaning.html.

Conway, Bobby. *Doubting Toward Faith: The Journey to Confident Christianity*. Eugene, OR: Harvest House, 2015.

Diederich, F. Remy. "Forgiveness Quotes by Desmond Tutu." Readingremy.com. Mar. 6, 2023. https://www.readingremy.com/blog/2012/03/06/forgiveness-quotes-by-desmond-tutu.

Evans, Rachel Held. *Searching for Sunday: Loving, Leaving, and Finding the Church*. Nashville: Nelson, 2015. Kindle.

Franke, John R. *Missional Theology: An Introduction*. Grand Rapids: Baker, 2020. Kindle.

Garcia-Navarro, Lulu. "Student Film 'Chuj Boys of Summer' Shines Gentle, Poetic Light on Home." Interview with Max Walker-Silverman. *Weekend Edition Sunday*, NPR, July 4, 2021.

Gorman, Michael J. *Becoming the Gospel: Paul, Participation, and Mission*. Grand Rapids: Eerdmans, 2015. Kindle.

Gumbel, Nicky. "The strength of your faith is not measured by the absence of doubt, but by the faithfulness of your life in the face of doubt." Twitter. June 20, 2016. https://x.com/nickygumbel/status/744987739385401344.

Hamm, Terrance L. "Reversing the Residual Effects of Redlining." National League of Cities, Mar. 29, 2019.

Harper, Lisa Sharon. *The Very Good Gospel: How Everything Wrong Can Be Made Right*. New York: Waterbrook, 2016. Kindle.

InspiringQuotes. "Pierre Teilhard de Chardin Quotes." InspiringQuotes web site. https://www.inspiringquotes.us/quotes/4Zgv_6NtGKe1X.

BIBLIOGRAPHY

King, Martin Luther, Jr. *A Gift of Love: Sermons from* Strength to Love *and Other Preachings*. Boston: Beacon, 2012.

Leo XIII. *Graves de communi re*. Encyclical letter. Vatican website. Jan. 18, 1901. https://www.vatican.va/content/leo-xiii/en/encyclicals/documents/hf_l-xiii_enc_18011901_graves-de-communi-re.html.

Mandela, Nelson. *A Long Walk to Freedom*. Boston: Little, Brown, 1994.

Merriam-Webster. "Hate." https://www.merriam-webster.com/.

Mother Teresa of Calcutta. *In the Heart of the World: Thoughts, Stories & Prayers*, edited by Becky Benenate. Novato, CA: New World Library, 2010.

Musashi, Miyamoto. *The Book of Five Rings: Adapted for the Contemporary Reader*. Translated by James Harris. Independently published, 2022.

Nerburn, Kent. *Make Me an Instrument of Your Peace*. San Francisco: HarperCollins, 1999.

Owensby, Jake. *Looking for God in Messy Places: A Book About Hope; How to Find It. Practice It. Grow in It*. Nashville: Abingdon, 2021. Kindle.

Renoux, Christian. "The Origin of the Peace Prayer of St. Francis." The Franciscan Archive. https://www.franciscan-archive.org/franciscana/peace.html.

Rohr, Richard. *Falling Upward: A Spirituality for the Two Halves of Life*. Danvers, MA: Jossey-Bass, 2011.

Soerens, Tim. *Everywhere You Look: Discovering the Church Right Where You Are*. Downers Grove, IL: InterVarsity, 2020. Kindle.

SpiritualRay. "Profound Christian Quotes and Sayings That'll Leave You Blessed." https://spiritualray.com/christian-quotes-sayings.

Stone, Bryan. *Evangelism After Christendom: The Theology and Practice of Christian Witness*. Grand Rapids: Brazos, 2007. Kindle.

Tizon, Al. *Whole and Reconciled: Gospel, Church, and Mission in a Fractured World*. Grand Rapids: Baker Academic, 2018. Kindle.

Walker-Silverman, Max, dir. *Chuj Boys of Summer*. On *Weekend Edition* Student Film Showcase, NPR, July 31, 2021. https://www.npr.org/2021/07/04/1010905630/weekend-edition-student-film-showcase-watch-standout-student-films.

Wells, Sam. "The Discipline of Joy." Duke University Chapel, 2010. https://chapel.duke.edu/sites/default/files/documents/sermons/April4The DisciplineofJoy.pdf.

Wright, N. T. *The Case for the Psalms: Why They Are Essential*. New York: HarperOne, 2013.

Yancey, Philip. *Reaching for the Invisible God: What Can We Expect to Find?* Grand Rapids: Zondervan, 2000.

www.ingramcontent.com/pod-product-compliance
Lightning Source LLC
Chambersburg PA
CBHW071738090426
42738CB00011B/2516